Access 2000

Stephen Morris

QUICK FIX

TEACH YOURSELF BOOKS

For UK orders: please contact Bookpoint Ltd, 130 Milton Park, Abingdon, Oxon OX14 4SB. Telephone: (44) 01235 827720, Fax: (44) 01235 400454. Lines are open 9.00 - 6.00, Monday to Saturday, with a 24-hour message answering service. E-mail: orders@bookpoint.co.uk

British Library Cataloguing in Publication Data
A catalogue record for this title is available from the British Library.

First published 2001 by Hodder Headline Plc, 338 Euston Road, London, NW1 3BH.

Typeset by Butford Technical Publishing, Birlingham, Worcs.
Printed in Great Britain for Hodder & Stoughton Educational, a division of Hodder Headline Plc, 338 Euston Road, London NW1 3BH by Cox & Wyman, Reading, Berkshire.

Impression number   10 9 8 7 6 5 4 3
Year   2006 2005 2004 2003 2002

Contents

Starting Access 2000

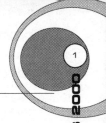

Load Access 2000

You can run Access in a similar way to any other Windows application:

1 Click on ▓Start.

2 Move the pointer to the **Programs** option.

3 Move the pointer across to **Microsoft Access** and click.

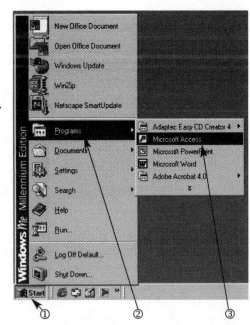

Create a blank Access database

When you load Access from the **Start** menu, you are given options for creating a new database or opening an existing database.

To create a blank database:

1 Click on **Blank Access database**.

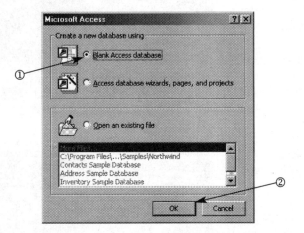

2 Click on **OK**. The File New Database dialog box is displayed.

3 Select the directory in which the database is to be stored or create a new directory.

4 Type a filename.

Existing directory ③ New directory

5 Click on **Create**.

The main Access window is displayed.

Display the Access window

The Access display contains all the usual Windows components. The main Access window includes the database window, where database objects are created and viewed.

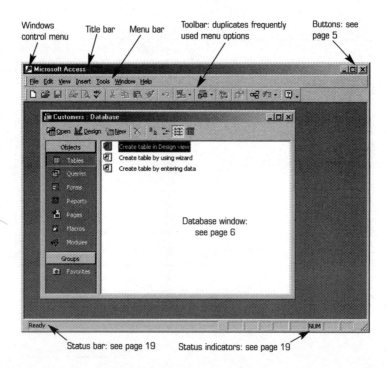

Windows control menu

Title bar

Menu bar

Toolbar: duplicates frequently used menu options

Buttons: see page 5

Database window: see page 6

Status bar: see page 19

Status indicators: see page 19

Resize the windows

The Access window can be maximized, minimized or closed.
Information from the database is displayed in a database
window, inside the main Access window; this window can also
be maximized (so that it fills the Access window), reduced in
size, minimized or closed.

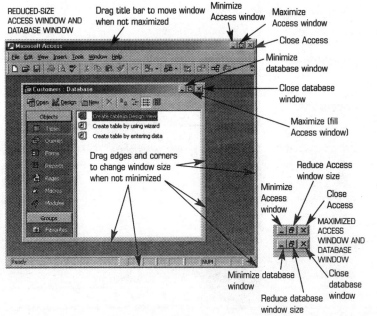

REDUCED-SIZE ACCESS WINDOW AND DATABASE WINDOW

Drag title bar to move window when not maximized

Minimize Access window

Maximize Access window

Close Access

Minimize database window

Close database window

Maximize (fill Access window)

Drag edges and corners to change window size when not minimized

Reduce Access window size

Minimize Access window

Close Access

MAXIMIZED ACCESS WINDOW AND DATABASE WINDOW

Minimize database window

Reduce database window size

Close database window

Use the database window

The database window contains all the *objects* that make up your database: tables (which store the data), forms (where data is entered), reports, queries etc.

• The left-hand pane of the window lists the types of object. Click on an item and the objects of that type are listed in the main part of the window.

• Below the object types, the **Groups** section allows you to group objects together.

• The buttons below the title bar provide shortcuts to standard operations.

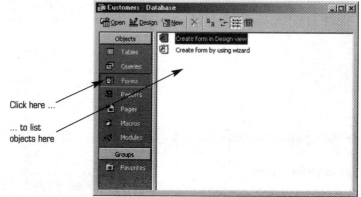

Click here ...

... to list
objects here

Close Access

Close Access in any of the following ways:

• Click on the ☒ button in the main window.

Click here

• From the **File** menu, select **Exit** (or press **[Alt] [F] [X]**).

Click here ...

Microsoft Access

File Edit View Insert Tools Window Help

New...	Ctrl+N
Open ...	Ctrl+O
Get External Data	
Close	
Save	Ctrl+S
Save As...	
Export...	
Page Setup...	
Print Preview	
Print ...	Ctrl+P
Send To	
Database Properties	

1 Customers
2 C:\Program Files\Microsoft Office 97\Office\Samples\Northwind
3 Contacts Sample Database
4 Address Sample Database

Exit

... then here

• Select **Close** from the control menu or press **[Alt] + [F4]**.

Click here ...

... then here

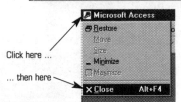

Microsoft Access

- Restore
- Move
- Size
- Minimize
- Maximize
- X Close   Alt+F4

On-line Help

Use the Office Assistant

The Office Assistant is an interactive help tool, which appears on
your screen when you first start Access. (If the Assistant is not
visible, select **Show the Office Assistant** from the **Help** menu.)

You can use the Assistant to
answer a particular query.

1 Click
anywhere on
the Assistant.
You are asked
what you want
to do.

2 Type a
query into the
box.

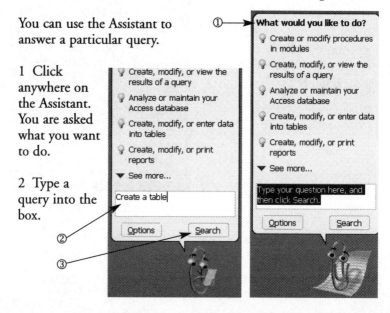

3 Click on **Search**. A list of possible matching topics is shown. If necessary, click on **See more** to list further topics.

4 Click on one of the topics. The Help window is displayed.

5 Click on the ☒ button to close the Help window.

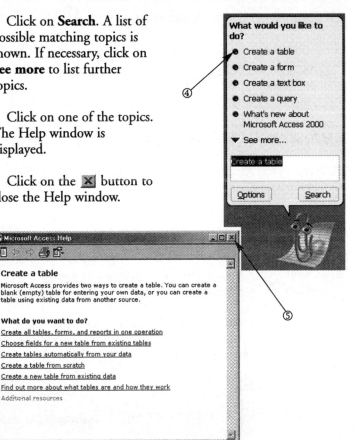

What would you like to do?
- Create a table
- Create a form
- Create a text box
- Create a query
- What's new about Microsoft Access 2000
- See more...

Create a table

| Options | Search |

🗒 Microsoft Access Help

Create a table

Microsoft Access provides two ways to create a table. You can create a blank (empty) table for entering your own data, or you can create a table using existing data from another source.

What do you want to do?

Create all tables, forms, and reports in one operation

Choose fields for a new table from existing tables

Create tables automatically from your data

Create a table from scratch

Create a new table from existing data

Find out more about what tables are and how they work

Additional resources

Show the Office Assistant

If the Office Assistant does not appear on your screen, or has been turned off completely, display it by selecting **Show the Office Assistant** from the **Help** menu.

Hide the Office Assistant

To remove the Office Assistant from your screen, select **Hide the Office Assistant** from the **Help** menu.

Turn off the Office Assistant

After hiding the Office Assistant a few times, you are given the option to turn off the feature completely.

You can also turn the Assistant off at any other time.

1 Click on the Office Assistant.

2 Click on **Options**.

3 Click on the box next to **Use the Office Assistant** (to remove the tick).

Change the way the Office Assistant works

You can change various options that affect the operation of the Assistant or the type of information it provides.

1 Click on the Office Assistant.

2 Click on the **Options** button.

3 On the **Options** tab, click on the check boxes to turn features on or off.

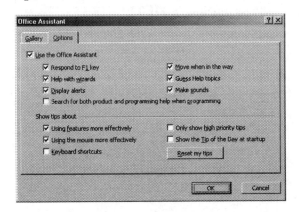

4 On the **Gallery** tab, select a different animation.

5 Click on **OK**.

Display the Help window

You can get on-line help directly from the Access Help program.

1 Turn off the Office Assistant completely (see above).

2 From the **Help** menu, select **Microsoft Access Help**.

   OR

   Press function key **[F1]**.

   OR

   Click on the 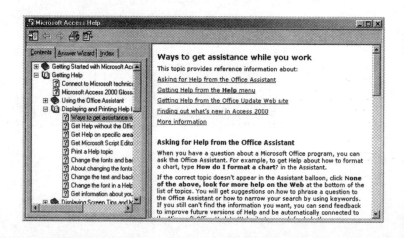 button on the toolbar.

Select a help topic

The Access help topics are arranged in a series of books, some of which contain other books.

- Click on the ⊞ symbol to open a book.

- Click on the ⊟ symbol to close a book.

- Click on a topic to display the corresponding help text.

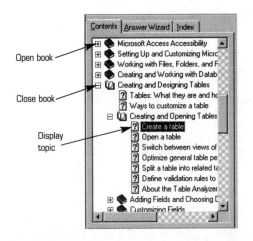

Jump to a related topic

From within the help text, you can jump to related help topics.

• Click on underlined text to jump to help relating to that phrase.

• Click on coloured (but not underlined) text to see a description of that phrase.

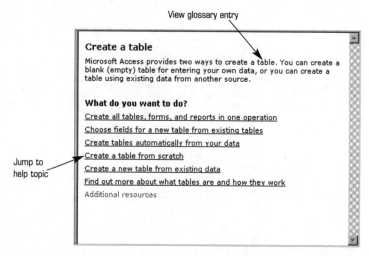

View glossary entry

Create a table

Microsoft Access provides two ways to create a table. You can create a blank (empty) table for entering your own data, or you can create a table using existing data from another source.

What do you want to do?

Create all tables, forms, and reports in one operation

Choose fields for a new table from existing tables

Create tables automatically from your data

Create a table from scratch

Create a new table from existing data

Find out more about what tables are and how they work

Additional resources

Jump to help topic

When you have viewed a topic once, the links to that topic are shown as purple rather than blue text.

Search for help with the Answer Wizard

You can search for help on a particular subject in two ways. The first method is similar to the Office Assistant approach:

1 Click on the **Answer Wizard** tab on the Help window.

2 Type a query in the upper box.

3 Click on the **Search** button.

4 Click on one of the topics in the lower box.

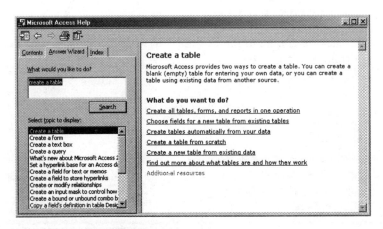

Search for help using the index

The help index lists key words and phrases in the help text.

1 Click on the **Index** tab in the Help window.

2 Type a word in the top box.

   OR

   Start typing a word and then click on the required keyword in the middle box.

3 Click on the **Search** button.

4 Click on a topic in the bottom box.

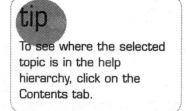

tip

To see where the selected topic is in the help hierarchy, click on the Contents tab.

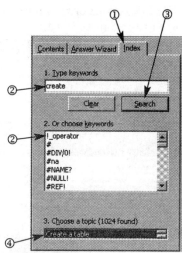

Use the Help window options

The buttons at the top of the Help window allow you to move around the help topics and perform other operations. You can:

- Hide (or redisplay) the left-hand pane, containing the tabs.

- Go back to the previous help topic you selected.

- Go forward again to the next help topic.

- Print the current help topic.

- List other help options.

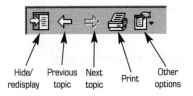

Hide/   Previous   Next   Print   Other
redisplay topic   topic   options

Use other help facilities

Access provides some other useful facilities that help you use the program:

• If you place the pointer over a toolbar button, after a short pause a label pops up to tell you what the button is.

• For more information about any object on the Access display, select **What's This** from the **Help** menu and then click on the object.

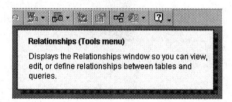

• For information from Microsoft on the Internet, select **Office on the Web** from the **Help** menu.

• For version number and product ID information, select **About Microsoft Access** from the **Help** menu.

Use the status bar

The status bar at the bottom of the worksheet window displays messages as you are working with Access.

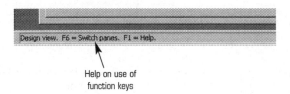

Design view. F6 = Switch panes. F1 = Help.

Help on use of
function keys

The right-hand side of the bar has a number of indicators that give you information about your computer.

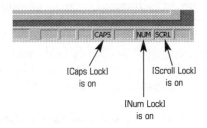

CAPS   NUM SCRL

[Caps Lock]
is on

[Scroll Lock]
is on

[Num Lock]
is on

Creating a Table

Design a table

The following terminology is used when working with Access databases:

• A database consists of a number of related *tables*. Each table contains data of one type (for instance, customer details or company details).

• A table contains a number of *records*. A record contains one set of data (for example, the data for one customer or one company). The structure of each record is the same within a table; the record structure varies from one table to another.

• The record is subdivided into *fields*. Each field contains one item of data, of a particular type (for instance, a field may be used to hold the customer's name or the company's fax number).

In this way, a table forms a rectangular grid of data, where each row is a record and each column contains the data for one field.

Fields

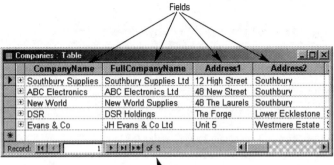

Companies : Table			
CompanyName	**FullCompanyName**	**Address1**	**Address2**
Southbury Supplies	Southbury Supplies Ltd	12 High Street	Southbury
ABC Electronics	ABC Electronics Ltd	48 New Street	Southbury
New World	New World Supplies	48 The Laurels	Southbury
DSR	DSR Holdings	The Forge	Lower Ecklestone
Evans & Co	JH Evans & Co Ltd	Unit 5	Westmere Estate

Record: 1 of 5

Tables

Contacts : Table				
ContactName	**ContactFullName**	**CompanyNam**	**Telephone**	**Ext**
J K Evans	John K Evans	Evans & Co	07908 206989	
J Williams	John Williams	Southbury Supp	02095 289780	242
M Evans	Mark Evans	Southbury Supp	02095 289780	297
N James	Nigella James	DSR	02095 650737	
R Fletcher	Ron Fletcher	New World	02095 556400	
T Smith	Tom Smith	ABC Electronic	02095 371206	

Record: 6 of 6

Records

Create a table

Access offers you three methods for creating a table:

- Design view: specify the fields that make up each record.

- Table Wizard: a series of steps to guide you through the process of building a table based on commonly used fields.

- By entering data: Access creates the table from data that you enter.

The fastest way to create a table is to use the Table Wizard or generate the table from entered data. However, you will have more control over the ultimate design of the table (and therefore have to make fewer modifications later) if you create the table in Design view.

tip

If you choose to use the Table Wizard or create the table from entered data, you can modify the table later using Design view.

Create a table by data entry

To create a table based on data that you enter directly:

1 In the database window, click on the **Tables** object and double-click on **Create table by entering data**.

2 A blank table is displayed in Datasheet view. Type a complete record into the first row, putting one item of data in each column. Type further records if required.

3 Click on the ▣ button on the Datasheet view window. Click on **Yes** when asked if you want to save the table.

4 Type a name for the table (avoiding the use of spaces) and click on **OK**.

5 A message is displayed stating that a primary key is needed. At this stage, click on **No**. (For information about primary keys, see page 34.)

The new table is added to the list on the right-hand side of the database window.

Access determines the type of each field from the data you have entered. You will need to check these types and change the names of the fields; see page 42 for more information.

Create a table in Design view

To create a table from scratch:

1 In the database window, click on the **Tables** object and double-click on **Create table in Design view**.

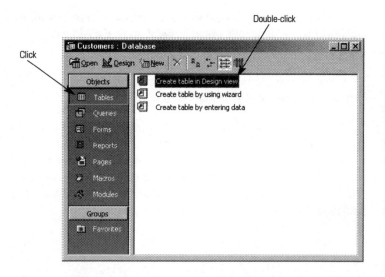

A blank table is displayed in Design view. Each row in the window defines one field in your table.

2 Type the name of the first field. The name can be up to 64 characters long, containing most characters except full stops (.), exclamation marks (!) and square brackets ([]). Although you can include spaces, it is best not to do so. (Spaces can cause problems later if the field has to be included in any program instructions.)

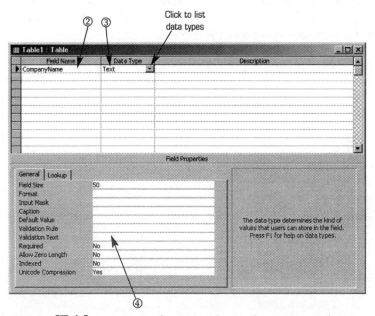

3 Press **[Tab]** to move to the **Data Type** column. From the drop-down list, choose the type of data to be held in the field.

4 If necessary, change the defaults for the field listed in the bottom half of the window. (For more information about data types and their properties, see page 42.)

5 Press **[Tab]** to move to the **Description** column. Enter any information needed to help users decide what to enter in the field. The description is displayed on the status bar when users are entering data in the field.

6 Press **[Enter]** or **[Tab]** to move down to the next row.

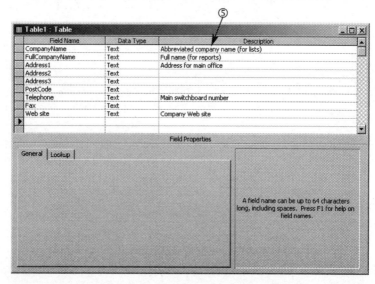

7 Repeat steps 2 to 6 for each field in the table.

8 Click on the ✗ button on the Design view window. Click on **Yes** when asked if you want to save the table.

9 Type a name for the table (avoiding the use of spaces) and click on **OK**.

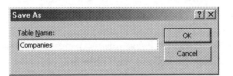

10 A message is displayed stating that a primary key is needed. At this stage, click on **No**. (For information about primary keys, see page 34.)

The new table is added to the list on the right-hand side of the database window.

Create a table using the Table Wizard

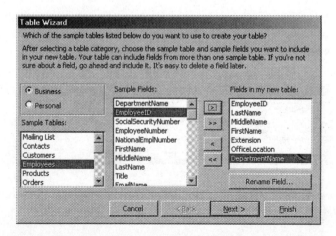

The Table Wizard guides you through the process of creating a table; this is a useful method if your table is made up of commonly used fields. The wizard can also be used as the starting point for creating a more complex table.

1 In the database window, click on the **Tables** object and double-click on **Create table by using wizard**.

2 Choose between **Business** or **Personal** to decide what sort of fields are displayed. Click on a **Sample Table** and then on one of the **Sample Fields**. Click on the top button to add the field to

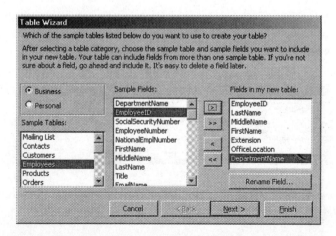

the table or the button below to
add all fields. The other two
buttons remove one or all fields
from the table. Repeat this
process with other tables and
fields until you have selected all
the fields you want. Click on
Next.

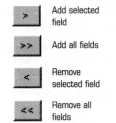

>	Add selected field
>>	Add all fields
<	Remove selected field
<<	Remove all fields

3 Type a name for the table (avoiding the use of spaces). Decide
whether or not you want Access to add a primary key (see page
34). Click on **Next**.

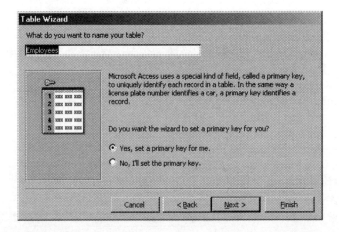

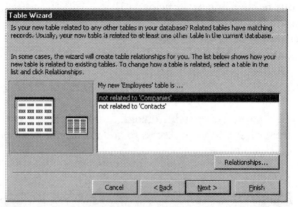

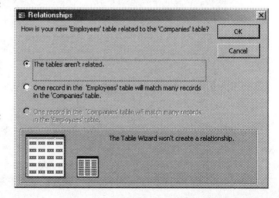

4 Decide whether the new table is related to existing tables (see page 112 for more information).

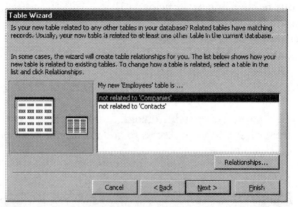

For each table that is related, click on the **Relationships** button and then choose the appropriate relationship type and click on **OK**. Click on **Next** when you have finished.

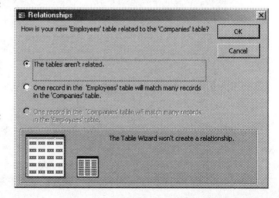

5 Finally, decide what you want to happen when the wizard has finished creating the table. Select one of the options and click on **Finish**.

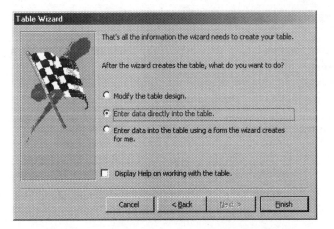

The wizard gives you three options:

• Modify the table design immediately by opening the Design view.

• Start entering data by opening the Datasheet view.

• Allow the wizard to create a simple data-entry form and then start entering data into the table using the wizard's form.

Modifying a Table

View a table

The tables you create are listed in the database window when the **Tables** object is selected.

To view the structure of a table:

1 In the database window, click on the **Tables** object.

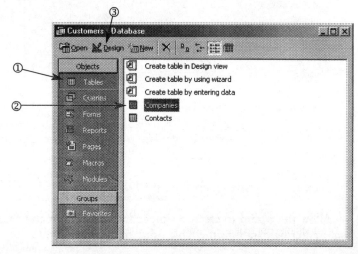

2 Click on the table name on the right-hand side of the window.

3 Click on the 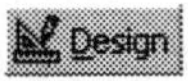 button. The Design view is displayed, with one row of information for each field in the table.

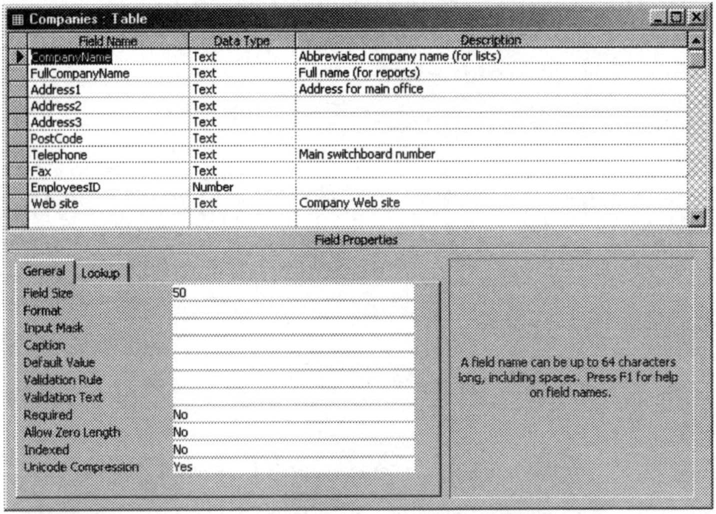
Companies : Table
Field Name
Data Type
Description
CompanyName
Text
Abbreviated company name (for lists)
FullCompanyName
Text
Full name (for reports)
Address1
Text
Address for main office
Address2
Text
Address3
Text
PostCode
Text
Telephone
Text
Main switchboard number
Fax
Text
EmployeesID
Number
Web site
Text
Company Web site
Field Properties
General
Lookup
Field Size
50
Format
Input Mask
Caption
Default Value
Validation Rule
Validation Text
Required
No
Allow Zero Length
No
Indexed
No
Unicode Compression
Yes
A field name can be up to 64 characters long, including spaces. Press F1 for help on field names.

tip

You now have two windows open, each with an icon on the Windows taskbar. You can switch between them by clicking on a visible part of a window or on the taskbar buttons.

Identify the primary key

The primary key uniquely identifies a record within a table.
Every table must have at least one field designated as the primary
key. The values given to this field must be different for every
record in the table. For example, the field could be a company
name or an employee number.

To identify the primary key:

1 In Design view, click on the field that is to be the primary
key.

2 Click on the 🔑 button. A key symbol is shown to the left
of the **Field Name**.

CompanyName is the primary
key for the Companies table

Primary key
symbol

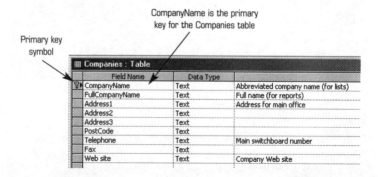

Field Name	Data Type	
CompanyName	Text	Abbreviated company name (for lists)
FullCompanyName	Text	Full name (for reports)
Address1	Text	Address for main office
Address2	Text	
Address3	Text	
PostCode	Text	
Telephone	Text	Main switchboard number
Fax	Text	
Web site	Text	Company Web site

Companies : Table

Change the primary key

You can change the primary key for a table.

1 In Design view, click on the field that is to be the new primary key.

2 Click on the 🔑 button. The key symbol is removed from the original field and shown to the left of the **Field Name** for the new primary key.

Change the primary key created by Access

When you create a table, you are asked if you want Access to create a primary key field for you. If you say **Yes**, Access adds a dummy field that is designated the primary key field. The **Data Type** for this field is set as **AutoNumber**, as a result of which each record is assigned a unique number when it is created.

To change the default primary key field:

1 In Design view, change the primary key, as described above.

2 If the default primary key field is no longer required, delete it (see page 37).

Assign multiple keys

If one field is not sufficient to identify a record uniquely, you can assign two or more primary keys. The combination of values in these fields must be different for each record.

1 In Design view, click on the first field.

2 Hold down **[Ctrl]** and click on the other primary fields.

3 Click on the 🔑 button.

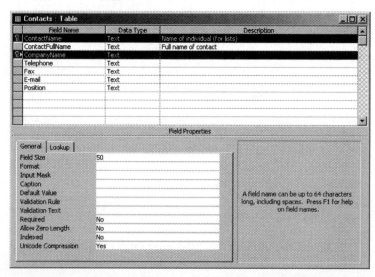

Add an AutoNumber field

If no set of fields is unique, records can be identified by a field whose value is automatically allocated by Access.

1 In Design view, insert a new field (see page 38).

2 Change the **Data Type** to **AutoNumber**.

3 Click on the button.

As records are created, the AutoNumber field is given a record number (which cannot be changed).

Remove a primary key

To remove a primary key (but leave the field in the record layout):

1 In Design view, click on the primary key field.

2 Click on the button. The key symbol is removed from next to the **Field Name**.

Insert a field

New fields can be added at the bottom of the record layout or inserted between existing fields.

To insert a field:

1 In Design view, click to the left of the field above which the new field is to be inserted.

2 Click on the button.

3 Type the **Field Name**, select the **Data Type** and provide a **Description** (if required).

4 Fill in any **Field Properties** required for the new field.

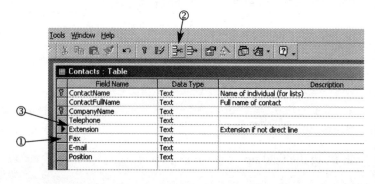

Delete a field

To delete a field:

1 In Design view, click to the left of the field that is to be
deleted.

2 Click on the 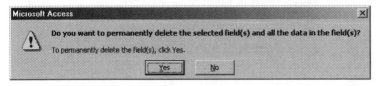 button or press **[Delete]**.

3 If data has already been entered for the field, a warning
message is displayed. Click on **Yes** to delete the field and all data
entered for it. (The data for other fields is not affected.)

Microsoft Access	
⚠	**Do you want to permanently delete the selected field(s) and all the data in the field(s)?**
	To permanently delete the field(s), click Yes.
	[Yes] [No]

Move a field

To move a field to a new position:

1 In Design view, click on the field to be moved (so that the
whole row is highlighted).

2 Drag the field up or down the list of fields to its new position.

Save the table changes

None of the changes you make to a table is saved until you close the Design view.

1 Click on the ✕ button on the Design view.

2 You are asked if you want to save the table. Click on **Yes** to save the table; click on **No** to abandon the changes; or click on **Cancel** to continue editing the table.

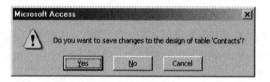

Add a table description

You can attach a brief description to each table.

1 In the database window, right-click on the table.

2 Select **Properties** from the drop-down menu.

3 Type a **Description** for the table and click on **OK**.

Rename a table

To rename a table:

1 In the database window, right-click on the table.

2 Select **Rename** from the drop-down menu.

3 Type a new name for the table and press **[Enter]**.

Delete a table

To delete a table:

1 In the database window, click on the table.

2 Click on the ✕ button on the toolbar.

3 Click on **Yes** to confirm that the table and its data are to be deleted.

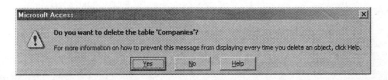

Defining Fields

Select the data type

The selection you make in the **Data Type** column places
restrictions on the type entry that can be made for that field.

Access supports the following data types:

• **Text**: any combination of characters (up to 255 characters in
length).

• **Memo**: long text items (up to 64,000 characters).

• **Number**: numeric values.

• **Date/Time**: date or time values.

• **Currency**: numeric values with a fixed number of decimal
places, typically used for currency amounts.

• **AutoNumber**: a number assigned by Access, either increasing
by 1 for each new record or allocated at random.

• **Yes/No**: a field with only two possible values.

- **OLE Object:** a link to another Windows file.

- **Hyperlink:** a link to another file or website.

- **Lookup Wizard:** a value selected from a list or another table. (The field is set up by the Lookup Wizard.)

Click to show list of data types

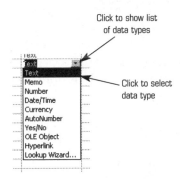

Click to select data type

tip

You can change the data type later, if necessary, even if there is already data in the table. (However, you will need to check that existing data is compatible with the new data type.)

Change field properties

Each field has a number of properties associated with it, such as the maximum size of the data or a default value. The properties are listed in the lower portion of the screen.

1 In Design view, click on a field.

2 Make the necessary changes to the properties.

When you click on another field the properties are stored away (though none of the changes you make is stored in the file until you close the Design view).

The properties that are included depend on the data type that has been selected.

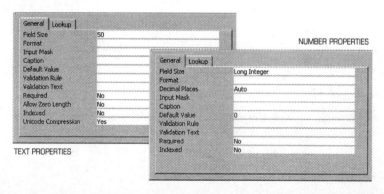

TEXT PROPERTIES

NUMBER PROPERTIES

Set the text field size

For text fields, you must specify the maximum number of characters that can be entered in the field.

1 In Design view, click on a text field.

2 In the **Field Properties** list, type the maximum length in the **Field Size** box.

Two other properties are relevant to text fields:

• **Allow Zero Length**: if set to **Yes**, allows the field to store a string of zero length, rather than the special **Null** value usually stored by Access for empty fields. This option is sometimes useful when writing Visual Basic programs.

• **Unicode Compression**: if set to **Yes**, the text uses less space when storing normal (ASCII) characters, even though the field is capable of storing any Unicode character.

tip

If the text field is a required field (see page 59) and Allow Zero Length is set to Yes, users can enter a space in the field; this is stored as a zero-length string.

Set the number field size

DEFINING FIELDS

For number fields, you must specify the type of number to be stored and its maximum size.

1 In Design view, click on a number field.

2 In the **Field Properties** list, click on the **Field Size** box.

3 Click on the arrow on the right of the box, so that the drop-down list of possible sizes is displayed. Click on an item in this list.

4 Set other properties, as necessary.

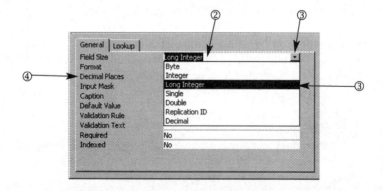

Access supports the following numeric field sizes:

- **Byte**: whole number between 0 and 255 (requires 1 byte storage space).

- **Integer**: whole number between -32,768 and 32,767 (2 bytes).

- **Long Integer**: whole number, up to nine digits long (4 bytes).

- **Single**: decimal value (4 bytes).

- **Double**: decimal value, with more significant figures allowed, giving greater precision in calculations (8 bytes).

- **Decimal**: decimal value, with fixed number of decimal places (12 bytes).

- **Replication ID**: unique identifier (16 bytes).

For Decimal fields, you should also specify the following properties:

- **Precision**: the number of digits stored for the value.

- **Scale**: the number of digits after the decimal point.

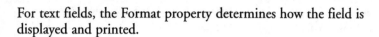

Format a text field

For text fields, the Format property determines how the field is displayed and printed.

1 In Design view, click on a text field.

2 In the **Field Properties** list, click on the **Format** box.

3 Type a format code (see below).

4 Press **[Enter]**.

The format codes can include the following symbols:

!	The text is left aligned.
<	Display in lower case letters.
>	Display in capitals.
" "	Always display any text in the quotes.
\	Display the character that follows.
@	A character is required.
&	A character is not required.
*	Remaining space is filled with the character that follows (e.g. *- fills the space with dashes).

A few other rules may apply when constructing a format:

• The code can consist of two parts, separated by a semi-colon(;). In that case, the second part gives the format for a Null value.

• You can specify that the text is to be displayed in a certain colour by placing the colour in square brackets (e.g. '[red]' to display the field in red).

• Spaces can be included in the format and will display as spaces.

For example, the following format could be used for a telephone number:

(@@@@) @@@@@@

tip

The format that you enter here only determines the way the text is displayed. It has no effect on how the text is stored in the database. For example, text in quotes is not stored with the data.

Format a number or currency field

For number and currency fields, the Format property determines how the number is displayed and printed.

1 In Design view, click on a number or currency field.

2 In the **Field Properties** list, click on the **Format** box.

3 Click on the arrow on the right of the box and select a format from the drop-down list.

    OR

    Type a format code (see below).

4 Press **[Enter]**.

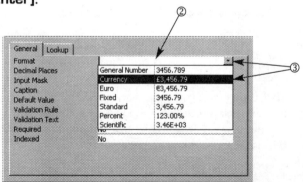

The format codes can include the following symbols:

#	Display a digit (if there is one).
0	Display a digit or zero.
.	Display a decimal point.
,	Display a thousands separator.
%	Display as percentage (value is multiplied by 100).
" "	Always display any text in the quotes.
£	Display a pound symbol (other currency symbols may also be used).

You can specify that a number is to be displayed in a certain colour by placing the colour in square brackets (e.g. '[red]' to display the value in red).

The format may have up to four sections, separated by semi-colons (;). There is one section for each of the following types of value:

- Positive numbers
- Negative numbers
- Zero
- Null values

For example:

> #,##0.00;[red]#,##0.00;"-";"-"

This displays at least one digit before the decimal place and always has exactly two digits after it. Thousands separators are used for each block of three digits. Negative numbers are shown in red and zero or null values display as a dash.

Enter format code, using up to four sections

General	Lookup
Format	#,##0.00;[Red]#,##0.00;"-";"-"
Decimal Places	Auto
Input Mask	
Caption	
Default Value	0
Validation Rule	
Validation Text	
Required	No
Indexed	No

Format a date/time field

For date and time fields, the Format property determines how the date/time is displayed and printed.

1 In Design view, click on a date/time field.

2 In the **Field Properties** list, click on the **Format** box.

3 Click on the arrow on the right of the box and select a format from the drop-down list.

> **OR**

Type a format code. There are a large number of characters that can be included in the code to determine exactly how dates and times are displayed. See the on-line help for a full list.

4 Press **[Enter]**.

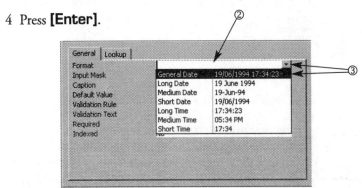

Add an input mask

For text and date/time fields, you can limit the way in which the user enters data. This is done by specifying an input mask, which provides a number of *placeholders* where individual characters can be entered.

1 In Design view, click on a text or date/time field.

2 In the **Field Properties** list, click on the **Input Mask** box.

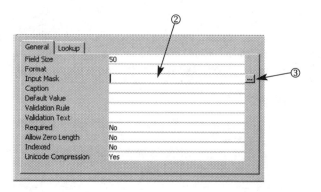

3 Click on the ▦ button to load the Input Mask Wizard. If you have not used this wizard before, you may have to load the Office CD so that the program can be installed. You will also be given the opportunity to save any changes made to the table.

4 Click on one of the input masks in the list. You can see how the mask will work by typing some sample data in the **Try It** box. When you are satisfied with the mask, click on **Next**.

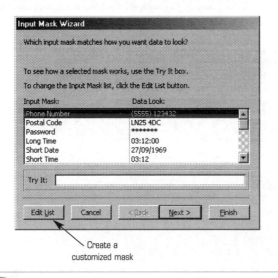

Input Mask Wizard

Which input mask matches how you want data to look?

To see how a selected mask works, use the Try It box.

To change the Input Mask list, click the Edit List button.

Input Mask:	Data Look:
Phone Number	(5555) 123432
Postal Code	LN25 4DC
Password	*******
Long Time	03:12:00
Short Date	27/09/1969
Short Time	03:12

Try It:

Edit List   Cancel   < Back   Next >   Finish

Create a customized mask

tip

The Password input mask is useful for entering sensitive data (such as passwords). Anything typed into the field is stored as it is typed but is displayed as asterisks.

5 Make any necessary changes to the mask to make it suit the data that will be entered for the field. Choose the character to be used as a placeholder. Test the mask by typing some sample data in the **Try It** box. Click on **Next** when you are satisfied with the mask.

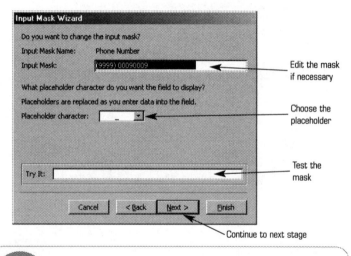

Edit the mask if necessary

Choose the placeholder

Test the mask

Continue to next stage

tip

At any stage you can click on the Back button to go back to the previous stage; Finish to jump to the end of the process; or Cancel to abandon the input mask.

6 For some types of mask, you must decide whether the extra symbols in the mask are to be stored with the data, or just displayed when entering values. Click on the appropriate option and then on **Next**.

DEFINING FIELDS

Input Mask Wizard

How do you want to store the data?

○ With the symbols in the mask, like this:

   (4575) 45264683

● Without the symbols in the mask, like this:

   331525384267

Cancel   < Back   Next >   Finish

7 Click on **Finish** to complete the mask.

Add a caption

If you are planning to create forms for entering records, you can specify a caption for each field. The caption is the default text that appears next to the field on the form. The caption also appears at the top of the column in Datasheet view. If no caption is specified, Access uses the field name.

1 In Design view, click on a field.

2 In the **Field Properties** list, click on the **Caption** box.

3 Enter a caption. You can use any characters.

Specify a default value

You can specify a value that will be shown in the field for any new record. If the user does not replace this with a different value, the default value is stored in the record.

1 In Design view, click on a field.

2 In the **Field Properties** list, click on the **Default Value** box.

3 Enter a value, making sure that it is compatible with any format that has been specified for the field.

Identify required fields

In some cases, it is essential that a value is always given for a particular field. This field should be marked as a *required* field. Access will then force users to enter a value in the field for every record.

1 In Design view, click on a field.

2 In the **Field Properties** list, click on the **Required** box.

3 Click on the arrow on the right of the box and select **Yes** from the list.

Primary key fields should normally be identified as required fields.

If the table already has some records, you must check that all these records already have values in the required fields.

tip

You may want to specify a default value for required fields, so that it is easier for the user to ensure that a value is always entered in the field.

Validate an input value

The data type and input mask give you some control over the values that are input to a field. However, you can also specify more complex rules to be applied to the data. For example, you may want to ensure that an input value lies within a specified range.

1 In Design view, click on a field.

2 In the **Field Properties** list, click on the **Validation Rule** box.

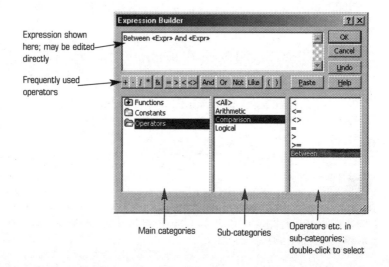

Expression shown here; may be edited directly

Frequently used operators

Main categories

Sub-categories

Operators etc. in sub-categories; double-click to select

3 Click on the 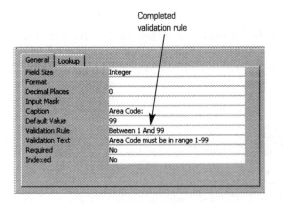 button to load the Expression Builder.

4 Use the buttons on the Expression Builder to define the validation rule.

5 Click on **OK**.

Completed
validation rule

General	Lookup
Field Size	Integer
Format	
Decimal Places	0
Input Mask	
Caption	Area Code:
Default Value	99
Validation Rule	Between 1 And 99
Validation Text	Area Code must be in range 1-99
Required	No
Indexed	No

The validation rule can be as simple or complex as you like. For example, 'Between 1 and 99' ensures that the input value is greater than zero and less than 100.

You should enter a corresponding message in the **Validation Text** property. This message is displayed when a value is entered that is contrary to the validation rule.

Create an index

You can speed up the process of searching for records or sorting a table according to the contents of a field by indexing the field. Access maintains a list of the values stored in indexed fields.

1 In Design view, click on the field to be indexed.

2 In the **Field Properties** list, click on the **Indexed** box.

3 Click on the arrow on the right of the box and select one of the indexing options from the list.

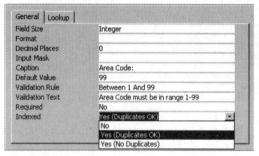

There are two options:

• **Yes (Duplicates OK)**: the same value may appear in more than one record.

• **Yes (No Duplicates)**: each value may appear in only one record.

Use the Lookup Wizard

The Lookup Wizard is used when you want to be able to select the value for a field from a list. The list can be either a set of standard values or the values held for a field in another table.

1 In Design view, click on the **Data Type** column for the required field.

2 Click on the arrow on the right of the column and select **Lookup Wizard**.

3 Follow the instructions given below, depending on whether you want a list based on another table (see page 66) or a list of standard values (see page 64).

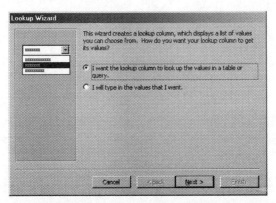

Look up values in a standard list

You can specify that a field can only accept entries selected from
a list of standard values.

1 In Design view, click on the **Data Type** column for the
required field and select **Lookup Wizard**.

2 Click on the second of the two options and then click on
Next.

3 Type the list of values, pressing **[Tab]** after each one. Then
click on **Next**.

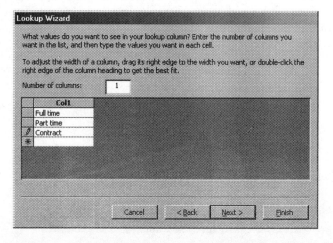

4 Give the list a name (the field name is offered as a default).
Click on **Finish**.

To view or edit the list:

1 In Design view, click on the **Data Type** column for the
lookup field.

2 In the **Field Properties** section, click on the **Lookup** tab.

3 Make any
necessary
changes.

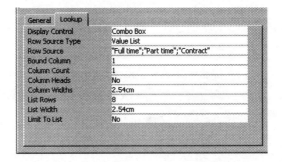

General	Lookup	
Display Control	Combo Box
Row Source Type	Value List
Row Source	"Full time";"Part time";"Contract"
Bound Column	1
Column Count	1
Column Heads	No
Column Widths	2.54cm
List Rows	8
List Width	2.54cm
Limit To List	No

tip

To ensure that the field can only hold values from the list,
change the Limit To List property to Yes; otherwise, you will
be able to enter values not in the list.

Look up values in a table

You can specify that a field can only accept entries from a field in some other table.

1 In Design view, click on the **Data Type** column for the required field and select **Lookup Wizard**.

2 Click on the first of the two options and then click on **Next**.

3 Click on the table that contains the list and then on **Next**.

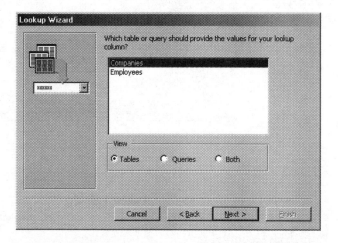

4 Click on one or more fields and select them using the button. Click on **Next**.

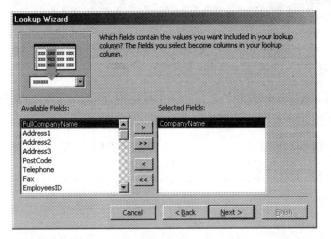

5 Set the width of the list by dragging the right-hand edge of the column. Click on **Next**.

6 Give the list a name (the field name is offered as a default). Click on **Finish**.

7 Click on **Yes** to save the table changes when asked to do so.

Details of the list are shown in the **Lookup** tab in the **Field Properties** section of the window.

Editing Records in Datasheet View

Open a table in Datasheet view

The simplest way to add records to your database is to open a table in Datasheet view.

1 In the database window, click on the **Tables** object.

2 Double-click on the table name on the right-hand side of the window.

   OR

   Click on the table name and then on the 🔳 Open button.

The Datasheet view is displayed:

• The main part of the window displays the table, with a column for each field and a row for each record. Initially there is just one empty record.

• At the bottom of the window, on the left-hand side, there is a navigation bar, which you can use to select records.

• To the right of the navigation bar is a scroll bar. Use this to show fields that will not fit on the window.

Record 1

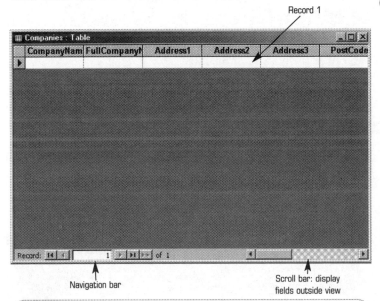

Navigation bar

Scroll bar: display fields outside view

tip

You now have two windows open, each with an icon on the Windows taskbar. You can switch between them by clicking on a visible part of a window or on the taskbar buttons.

Enter records into a table

To add a record to a table:

1 In Datasheet view, click on the first column in the blank record at the bottom of the table.

2 Type the value for the first field. A new blank record is added to the table, below the current record. Press **[Tab]** to move to the second field.

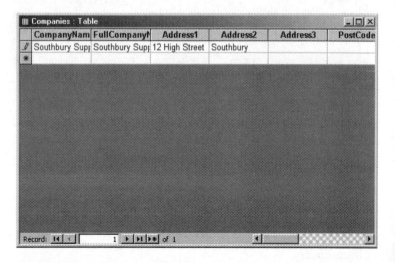

3 Type values into each of the other fields, pressing **[Tab]** after each one. When you have entered the last field, you are taken to the start of the next record.

4 Enter further records in the same way. The record number is shown in the navigation bar.

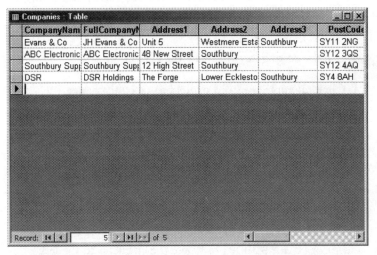

5 After entering all the records, click on the ☒ button in the Datasheet view to close the window.

Note that any data you enter is stored in the database immediately.

Edit a record in a table

To edit a record in a table:

1 In Datasheet view, use the scroll bars to find the record and field where the correction is to be made.

2 Click on the item that is to be corrected.

3 Use the editing keys to make the correction.

4 Click on another record or field to save the change.

You can edit an item in the following ways:

• Click on the text or number and move the vertical cursor to the point at which the correction is to be made.

• Type any characters to be inserted at the cursor position.

• Press **[Delete]** to delete the character to the right of the cursor or **[Backspace]** to delete the character to the left.

Select data for editing

You can select part of the data in any field or the entire field.

• To select one or more characters, click at the start of the text to be marked and drag the pointer to the end of the marked text.

• To select a whole word, double-click on the word.

• To select the entire field, click on the border to the left of the field.

CompanyNam	FullCompanyN	Address1	Address2	Address3	PostCode
Evans & Co	JH Evans & Co	Unit 5	Westmere Esta	Southbury	SY11 2NG
ABC Electronic	ABC Electronic	48 New Street	Southbury		SY12 3QS
Southbury Supp	Southbury Supp	12 High Street	Southbury		SY12 4AQ
DSR	DSR Holdings	The Forge	Lower Ecklesto	Southbury	SY4 8AH

Companies : Table

Click to select whole field

You can delete or replace the selected text:

• To delete the selection, click on **[Delete]** or **[Backspace]**.

• To replace the selection, type a new value.

Copy text within a field

Part of the contents of a field can be copied to another field.

1 In Datasheet view, mark the text to be copied.

2 From the **Edit** menu, select **Copy**.

   OR

   Press **[Ctrl]** and **[C]** together.

3 The value is now held in the Windows clipboard. Click on the field where the text is to be copied.

4 From the **Edit** menu, select **Paste**.

   OR

   Press **[Ctrl]** and **[V]** together.

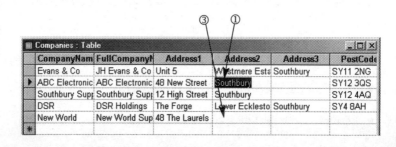

CompanyNam	FullCompanyN	Address1	Address2	Address3	PostCode
Evans & Co	JH Evans & Co	Unit 5	Westmere Esta	Southbury	SY11 2NG
ABC Electronic	ABC Electronic	48 New Street	Southbury		SY12 3QS
Southbury Supp	Southbury Supp	12 High Street	Southbury		SY12 4AQ
DSR	DSR Holdings	The Forge	Lower Ecklesto	Southbury	SY4 8AH
New World	New World Sup	48 The Laurels			

Copy a field

The contents of a field can be copied to another field.

1 Mark the field to be copied. (Click on the border to the left.)

2 From the **Edit** menu, select **Copy**.

   OR

   Press **[Ctrl]** and **[C]** together.

3 The value is now held in the Windows clipboard. Mark the field where the value is to be copied. (Click on the border.)

4 From the **Edit** menu, select **Paste**.

   OR

   Press **[Ctrl]** and **[V]** together.

③ ①

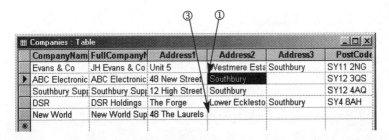

	CompanyNam	FullCompany!	Address1	Address2	Address3	PostCode
	Evans & Co	JH Evans & Co	Unit 5	Westmere Esta	Southbury	SY11 2NG
▶	ABC Electronic	ABC Electronic	48 New Street	Southbury		SY12 3QS
	Southbury Supp	Southbury Supp	12 High Street	Southbury		SY12 4AQ
	DSR	DSR Holdings	The Forge	Lower Eckllesto	Southbury	SY4 8AH
	New World	New World Sup	48 The Laurels			
*						

Copy a series of fields

The contents of a group of consecutive fields can be copied to another record.

1 In Datasheet view, mark the fields to be copied by clicking on the border to the left of the first cell and then dragging the pointer over the series of cells to be copied.

2 From the **Edit** menu, select **Copy**.

   OR

   Press **[Ctrl]** and **[C]** together.

   OR

   Right-click and select **Copy** from the pop-up menu.

3 Mark the fields where the values are to be copied. The number of new fields must match the number being copied.

4 From the **Edit** menu, select **Paste**.

   OR

   Press **[Ctrl]** and **[V]** together.

   OR

   Right-click and select **Paste** from the pop-up menu.

Copy one or more records

You can make a complete copy of one or more records. The copies can then be edited. (This can provide a fast way of generating records when the data is similar from one record to the next.)

1 In Datasheet view, mark the records to be copied by clicking on the row selector to the left of the first field. To mark several records, drag the pointer down the row selectors.

2 Press **[Ctrl]** and **[C]** together.

3 Click on the record selector for the blank record at the bottom of the table.

4 Press **[Ctrl]** and **[V]** together.

　　OR

Right-click and select **Paste** from the pop-up menu.

5 If copying multiple records, confirm the action by clicking on **Yes**.

Repeat previous copies

You can store clipboard data in memory even when you copy further items. Up to 12 sets of data are held in memory and can be copied to new locations (in Datasheet view).

Start by turning on the Clipboard toolbar:

1 From the **View** menu, select **Toolbars**.

2 Click on the **Clipboard** option.

Now, when you copy text, a field or a record, an icon is added to the toolbar. You can paste any of the copied items into any appropriate location:

1 Click on a field or mark a field or record.

2 Move the pointer over the Clipboard toolbar icons until you find the one you want.

3 Click on the icon.

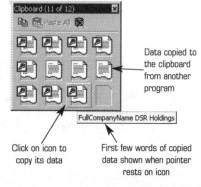

Data copied to the clipboard from another program

FullCompanyName DSR Holdings

Click on icon to copy its data

First few words of copied data shown when pointer rests on icon

You can turn off the toolbar by clicking on its ☒ button.

Cancel the last action

You can cancel the changes you have made to the current record in Datasheet view as follows:

- From the **Edit** menu, select **Undo**.

    OR

- Press **[Ctrl]** and **[Z]**.

The name of the Undo option varies, depending on the action that is to be undone. For example, after entering a field and moving to another field in the same record the option is **Undo Current Field/Record**; after moving to another record, the option becomes **Undo Saved Record**.

Delete one or more records

To delete one or more records:

1 In Datasheet view, click on the record selector to the left of the first record that is to be deleted. If you want to delete several records, drag the pointer over the record selectors for all the records to be deleted.

2 From the **Edit** menu, select **Delete Record**.

3 A warning message is displayed. Click on **Yes** to delete the record.

Note that you cannot undo this action.

Find a record

You can move to a different record in Datasheet view in the following ways:

• Use the cursor keys to move up and down the records. Each time you press one of the cursor keys, the record above or below becomes the current record.

• Use the vertical scroll bar to move up and down the table. Note that the current record does not change; to make a record the current record you must click on it.

• Use the buttons on the navigation bar at the bottom of the Datasheet view window.

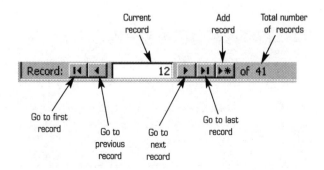

Find text in a record

You can search a table for records containing a specific value or item of text.

1 From the **Edit** menu, select **Find** or press **[Ctrl]** + **[F]**.

2 In the **Find What** box, type the text or value to search for.

3 Click on **Find Next**. The first field containing the specified text or value is selected.

4 Keep clicking on **Find Next** until you have found the record you are searching for.

5 Click on **Cancel**.

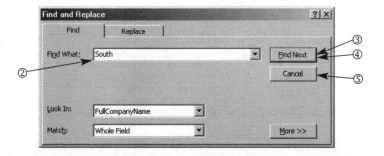

Modify a search

The search can be modified in the following ways:

• In the **Look In** box you can choose between searching the current field only or all fields.

• In the **Match** box, you can choose to search for fields where the search text is the complete entry, part of the entry or at the start of the entry.

• Click on the **More** button to display options for the direction of the search and whether the case of the text or the formatting of the field is checked.

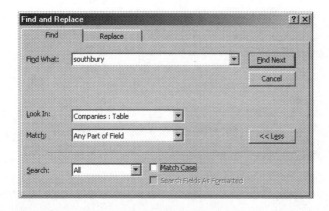

Replace one entry with another

You can search a table for a specific value or piece of text and then replace it with another entry.

1 From the **Edit** menu, select **Replace** or press **[Ctrl]** + **[H]**.

2 In the **Find What** box, type the text or value to search for.

3 In the **Replace With** box, type the text or value that is to replace the search value.

4 As for the **Find** option, choose the search criteria. (Additional criteria are displayed by clicking on the **More** button.)

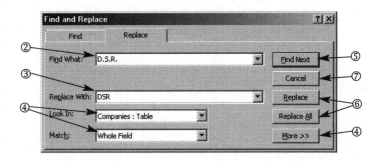

5 Click on **Find Next**. The first field containing the specified text or value is selected.

6 Click on **Replace** to replace the found value with the new value; **Replace All** to replace all occurrences throughout the table; or **Find Next** to move to the next occurrence without making any change. Repeat until all occurrences have been checked.

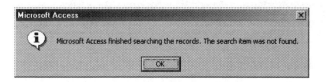

7 Click on **Cancel**.

You can also start the Replace option by clicking on the Replace tab in the Find and Replace dialog box. Fill in the 'Replace With' box and then continue as before.

Correct spelling mistakes

The Access spelling checker searches a table for words that are not included in its dictionary and gives you the opportunity to change them.

1 Move to the first field of the first record. (Press **[Ctrl]** + **[Home]** to jump straight to record 1.)

2 From the **Tools** menu, select **Spelling** or click on the ✓ button. The first incorrect spelling is displayed.

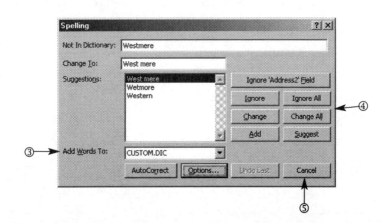

3 If necessary change the way the spelling check is carried out (see below).

4 Decide how to handle the word that has been found (see below). Each possible error is displayed in turn.

5 Continue with the spelling check until all words have been checked or stop at any time by clicking on **Cancel**. (You can also cancel the previous change you made by clicking on **Undo Last**.)

For each possible error that is identified, you have the following options:

• Click on **Ignore** to jump to the next error or **Ignore All** to ignore all future occurrences of this spelling. You can also ignore all occurrences in the current field.

• Click on **Change** to change the incorrect word for the suggested word or type your own correction in the **Change To** box and click on **Change**. Click on **Change All** to make the same change throughout the table.

• Click on **Add** to add the word that has been found to the custom dictionary; the word will not be identified in future.

• Click on **AutoCorrect** to add the word and its correction to the AutoCorrect list (see page 89).

Modify the spelling checker

The way the spelling check works can be changed by clicking on the **Options** button and then selecting options as follows:

• Click on **Always Suggest** to turn the suggestions off or on.

• Click on **From Main Dictionary Only** if you do not want suggestions to come from the custom dictionary.

• Click on **Words in UPPERCASE** to ignore any words entirely in capital letters.

• Click on **Words with Numbers** to ignore any words that contain numbers.

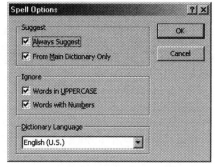

• Select the language for the spelling checker from the **Dictionary Language** box.

In the main Spelling dialog box, in the **Add Words To** field, select the name of the file to contain the custom dictionary. Words from this file are assumed to be correct. To start a new dictionary, type a new filename.

Make corrections automatically as you type

Access provides a feature whereby common errors can be corrected as you make entries in the table. The way the corrections are made can be viewed and changed by selecting **AutoCorrect** from the **Tools** menu.

The top four options make changes to capital letters as they are entered. Click on the **Exceptions** button to change the way these options work.

The bottom half of the dialog box lists words that are automatically changed. You can add new words to the list.

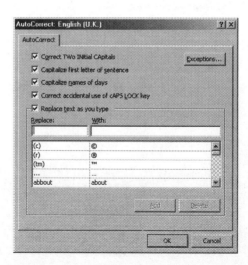

Modifying the Datasheet

Move a column

You can rearrange the columns in the table by moving one or more columns.

To move a column:

1 In Datasheet view, click on the field name at the top of the column so that the column is highlighted.

2 Drag the field name to its new position.

Click to select
the column

CompanyNam	FullCompanyI	Address1	Address2	Address3	Po
ABC Electronic	ABC Electronic	48 New Street	Southbury		SY12
DSR	DSR Holdings	The Forge	Lower Ecklesto	Southbury	SY4 8
Evans & Co	JH Evans & Co	Unit 5	Westmere Esta	Southbury	SY11
New World	New World Sup	48 The Laurels	Southbury		sdsd
Southbury Sup	Southbury Sup	12 High Street	Southbury		SY12

Companies : Table

Hide a column

You can temporarily hide a column.

1 In Datasheet view, right-click on the field name at the top of the column.

2 Select **Hide Columns** from the pop-up menu.

Show a hidden column

You can redisplay a column that was previously hidden.

1 In Datasheet view, select **Unhide Columns** from the **Format** menu.

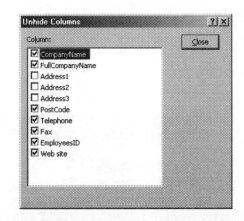

2 Click to the left of the hidden columns that are to be redisplayed.

3 Click on **Close**.

Freeze one or more columns

If you need to see one or more of the columns on the left while
you are working in fields further over to the right, you can freeze
the position of the left-hand columns so that they stay in view
all the times.

1 In Datasheet view, mark the columns that you want to freeze
by clicking on the field label at the top of the column (for a
single column) or dragging the pointer across several field labels
(for multiple columns).

2 From the **Format** menu, select **Freeze Columns**.

Now when you scroll across to the right, the frozen columns
remain visible.

Frozen column stays
visible on the left
even when scrolling
to the right

CompanyNam	Address2	Address3	PostCode	Telephone	
ABC Electronic	Southbury		SY12 3QS	02095 371206	
DSR	Lower Ecklesto	Southbury	SY4 8AH	02095 650737	
Evans & Co	Westmere Esta	Southbury	SY11 2NG	07908 206989	
New World	Southbury		SY13 5RW	02095 556445	
Southbury Supp	Southbury		SY12 4AQ	02095 289780	

Companies : Table

Unfreeze a column

Columns that have been frozen can be unfrozen, so that the
display moves freely again.

From the **Format** menu, select **Unfreeze All Columns**.

tip

When you freeze a column, it is moved to the left-hand side
of the table. Therefore, after unfreezing a column you may
need to move it again.

Insert a column

You can insert a column in Datasheet view; this is equivalent to adding a field in Design view.

1 Click on the field label of the column to the right of the point at which the new column is to be inserted.

2 Right-click on the highlighted column and select **Insert Column** from the pop-up menu.

A field called Field1 is added. The data type is set according to the data you enter. You can change the properties in Design view.

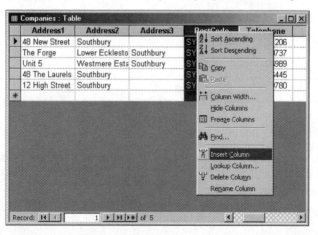

Rename a column

You can rename any field in Datasheet view.

1 Right-click on the field label and select **Rename Column**.

2 Type a new name for the column and press **[Enter]**.

Delete a column

An unwanted column can be deleted in Datasheet view. All data in that column will also be deleted.

1 Right-click on the field label and select **Delete Column**.

2 Click on **Yes** to confirm the deletion of the column and all its data.

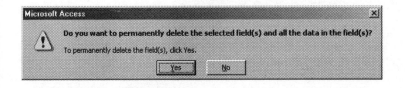

Change the width of a column

Each column in the table in Datasheet view is given a default width. You can set this width to any other value.

1 Right-click on the field label and select **Column Width**.

2 Type a new width and click on **OK**.

   OR

   Click on **Best Fit** to make the column width fit the widest item of data in the column.

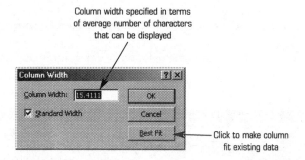

Column width specified in terms
of average number of characters
that can be displayed

Click to make column
fit existing data

Alternatively, if the exact width is not important, click on the border to the right of the field label and drag to the right or left.

Drag column border to change width

CompanyName	FullCompanyName	Address1	Address2	A
ABC Electronics	ABC Electronics Ltd	48 New Street	Southbury	
DSR	DSR Holdings	The Forge	Lower Ecklestone	So
Evans & Co	JH Evans & Co Ltd	Unit 5	Westmere Estate	So
New World	New World Supplies	48 The Laurels	Southbury	
Southbury Supplies	Southbury Supplies Ltd	12 High Street	Southbury	

Companies : Table

Record: 6 of 6

To change the width of several columns:

1 Drag the pointer across the column labels to mark the columns.

2 From the **Format** menu, select **Column Width**.

3 Enter a new width and click on **OK**.

   OR

   Click on **Best Fit**.

Change the height of a row

Each row in the table in Datasheet view is given a default height. You can set this height to any other value.

1 Right-click on the field label and select **Row Height**.

2 Type a new height and click on **OK**.

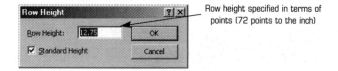

Row height specified in terms of points (72 points to the inch)

Alternatively, if the exact height is not important, click on the border between rows and drag up or down.

Drag to change height

Save the changes to the Datasheet view

The changes you make to the appearance of the Datasheet view (column order, hidden and frozen columns, column width and row height) can be saved when you close the view. The view will then look the same the next time you open it.

When you click on the ☒ button on the Datasheet view you are given the opportunity to save the changes.

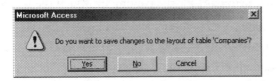

- Click on **Yes** to close the view and save the changes.

- Click on **No** to close the view without saving the changes.

- Click on **Cancel** to continue working in the view.

When you save the changes, this does not affect the data held in the table (which is saved whenever you move to a different record).

Sort a column

When you open a table in Datasheet view, the records are sorted in order of the values in the primary key field. If there is more than one key field, the second and subsequent keys are used for sorting those records for which the values for the first key are the same. (The sort is always carried out left to right.)

The records in the table can be sorted into order according to the contents of any other column.

1 Click on the field label for the column on which the sort is to be based.

2 Click on the ![ascending] button to sort the column into ascending (A to Z or numerically increasing) order.

OR

Click on the ![descending] button to sort into descending (Z to A or numerically decreasing) order.

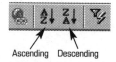

Ascending   Descending

When you close the Datasheet view, the sort order is saved along with other aspects of the layout.

Sort on several columns

The table can be sorted according to the contents of two or more fields.

1 Move the columns on which the sort is to be based so that they are next to each other. Check that they are in the right order (the sort is always performed left to right).

2 Mark the sort fields by dragging the pointer across their column labels.

3 Click on the ![button] button to sort the columns into ascending (A to Z or numerically increasing) order.

OR

Click on the ![button] button to sort into descending (Z to A or numerically decreasing) order.

Note that you can also activate the sort by right-clicking and selecting the appropriate sort option or by selecting **Sort** from the **Records** menu.

Display and hide toolbars

Access is supplied with a number of toolbars, containing buttons for performing a variety of tasks.

• To display a toolbar, from the **View** menu select **Toolbars** and then click on the required toolbar.

• To hide a toolbar, click on the toolbar's ⊠ button (if it is a 'floating' toolbar) or select **Toolbars** from the **View** menu and click on the toolbar name again.

Move a toolbar

Toolbars can be either 'docked' (where they are in a fixed position next to one edge of the Access window) or 'floating' (where they appear as separate windows within the main Access window).

• To change a docked toolbar into a floating toolbar, drag the vertical bar on the left-hand side of the toolbar into the middle of the Access window. Floating toolbars can be moved by dragging their title bars.

• To change a floating toolbar into a docked toolbar, drag the title bar to any edge of the Access window.

Show more buttons on a toolbar

When several toolbars are docked, there may not be enough room to display all the buttons on the toolbar. You can change the buttons that are shown.

1 Click on the downward-pointing arrow on the right of the toolbar and then click on **Add or Remove Buttons**.

2 Click on individual buttons to add or remove them.

Create a toolbar

New toolbars can be created to group together those buttons that you use most frequently.

1 From the
View menu,
select **Toolbars**
and click on the
Customize
option at the
bottom of the
list.

2 Click on the
Toolbars tab.

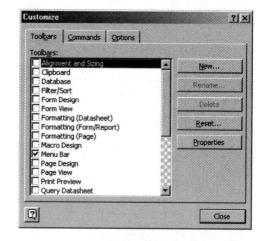

3 Click on the **New** button.

4 Type a name for the
toolbar and click on **OK**.

5 Click on the
Commands tab.

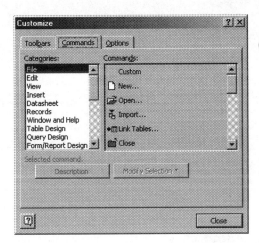

6 Click on an item
in the **Categories**
list.

7 Drag one or
more items from
the **Commands** list
onto the new
toolbar. Repeat for
other categories as
necessary.

8 Rearrange the selected buttons by dragging them within the
new toolbar.

9 Click on **Close**.

The new toolbar is added to the bottom of the **Toolbars** list.

Working with Files

Copy a database

You may want to make a copy of a database using a different name; for example, you may want to keep an original version of a database or use one database as the basis for another.

1 In Access, close the database.

2 In Windows Explorer, locate the directory where the database is stored and click on the database file (which will have an 'mdb' extension).

3 From the **Edit** menu, select **Copy**.

4 Open the directory where you want to store the copy. (You can also create the copy in the original directory.)

5 From the **Edit** menu, select **Paste**.

6 Rename the file if necessary. (Right-click on the file and select **Rename**.)

The original file is unchanged.

Store additional details

Access allows you to store additional information for each file, such as the title of the file, the author's name and other, general comments.

1 From the **File** menu, select **Database Properties**. The Properties dialog is displayed, with the **Author** and **Company** names taken from the computer's registry entries.

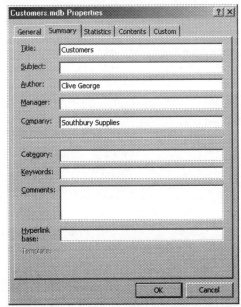

2 Fill in the other boxes. You can use the boxes for any purpose you like. (You can also change the **Author** and **Company**, if necessary.)

3 Click on **OK**.

Open or create a file when starting Access

When you start Access you are given options to create a new database or open an existing database.

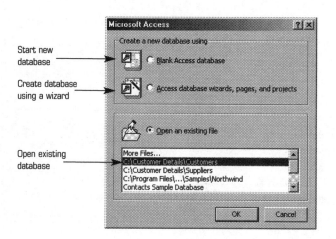

Start new database

Create database using a wizard

Open existing database

• Click on one of the options in the top half of the dialog box to create a database from scratch or use a wizard.

• Click on one of the recently used databases in the bottom half of the dialog box.

Load a database

To load an existing database when Access is already open:

1 From the **File** menu, select **Open**.

2 In the box at the top of the dialog, find the directory where the database is stored.

3 Click on the database, which will have an 'mdb' extension.

4 Click on **Open**. Note that you can only have one database open at a time.

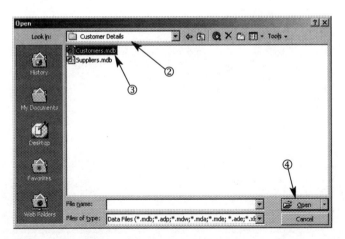

Create a new database

To create a new database while Access is open:

1 Click on the 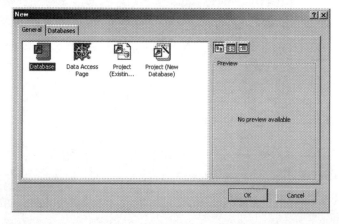 icon on the toolbar or select **New** from the **File** menu.

2 Click on the **Database** icon to create an empty database.

   OR

  Click on the **Databases** tab and then on a wizard icon to create a standard database.

3 Click on **OK**.

Close the database

When you have finished working with a database, you can close the file.

- From the **File** menu, select **Close**.

   OR

- Click on the ✕ button in the database window.

Click to close database

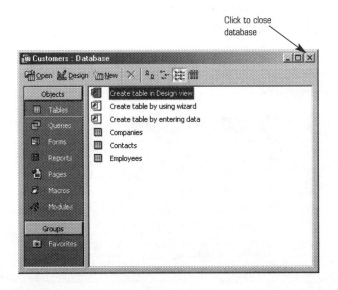

Display the Relationships window

There will usually be relationships between the tables in a database. For example, an employee's record may specify the department the employee works in and there may be data for each department in another table. The employee table is linked to the department table through the department name or other identifier. The Relationships window allows you to specify how tables are linked.

To display the Relationships window, select **Relationships** from the **Tools** menu.

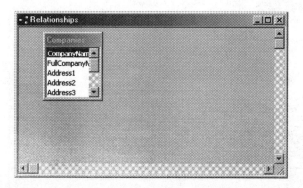

Add tables to the Relationships window

To add tables to the Relationships window:

1 From the **Relationships** menu, select **Show Table**.

   OR

   Click on the 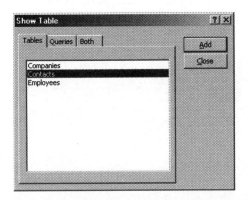 button.

2 Click on a table and then on **Add**. Repeat for each table you want to view and then click on **Close**.

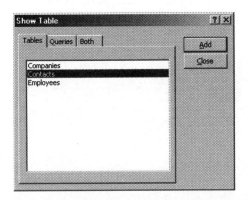

Each time you add a table, another small window is shown inside the Relationships window.

Modify the Relationships window display

You can change the appearance of the Relationships window:

• Drag the edges or corners of the window to change the window size.

• Drag the edges or corners of the small table windows to change their size; drag their title bars to move them within the Relationships window.

• Right-click on a table and select **Hide Table** to remove the table from the Relationships window. (The table itself is unaffected.)

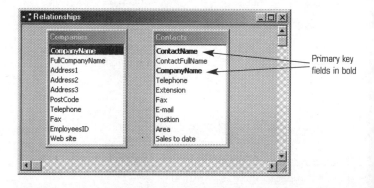

Primary key fields in bold

Save changes to the Relationships window

You can save the changes you have made to the layout of the Relationships window.

1 Right-click on a blank area of the Relationships window.

2 Select **Save Layout**.

The next time you open the Relationships window, the size, shape and contents will be as you saved them.

If you close the Relationships window without saving the layout changes you are prompted to do so.

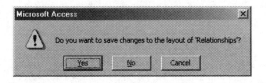

Click on **Yes** to save the layout or **No** to abandon the changes you have made. (**Cancel** allows you to continue working in the Relationships window.)

Create a relationship

If two fields in different tables contain the same items of data, you should create a link between them. Usually, a data field in one table will hold a value that is a key field in the other database.

1 From the **Relationships** menu, select **Edit Relationship**.

2 Click on the **Create New** button.

3 Choose the tables that are to be linked and the relevant field in each case. Click on **OK**.

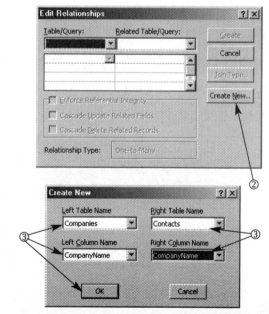

4 Click on the **Create** button.

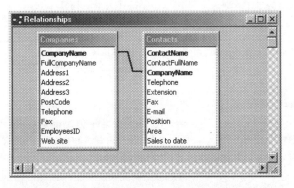

The new relationship is shown in the Relationships window as a
line joining the selected fields.

To change the fields that are linked in a relationship or alter other properties of the relationship:

1 In the Relationships window, right-click on the middle part of the link and select **Edit Relationship**.

OR

Double-click on the link.

2 Make the changes in the Edit Relationships dialog box.

3 Click on **OK**.

The **Relationship Type** in the Edit Relationships dialog box is shown as **One-To-Many**. This means that for each record in the first table there may be one or more records in the second table that have the same value in the selected field. For example, for each department there will be many employees.

tip

If you use the Lookup Wizard to set up a field and choose the option to look up the value in a table, a relationship is created automatically between the selected fields.

Show relationships

The Relationships window can show some or all relationships in
the database:

• To show the relationships for a particular table, click on the
table in the Relationships window and then select **Show Direct**
from the **Relationships** menu.

• To show all relationships in the database, select **Show All**
from the **Relationships** menu.

Delete a relationship

To delete a relationship:

1 In the **Relationships** window, right-click on the middle part
of the link.

2 Select **Delete**.

3 A warning message is displayed. Click on **Yes**.

Display a subdatasheet

If a relationship has been defined between two tables, you can view related records from Datasheet view.

1 Open a table in Datasheet view. If a field has a one-to-many relationship with a field in another table, a ⊞ button is shown next to the record.

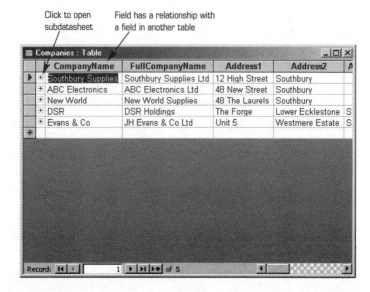

Click to open subdatasheet   Field has a relationship with a field in another table

2 Click on the ⊞ button to see the related records for that
value. The records are shown in a subdatasheet, where they can
be edited in the usual way.

Click to close
subdatasheet

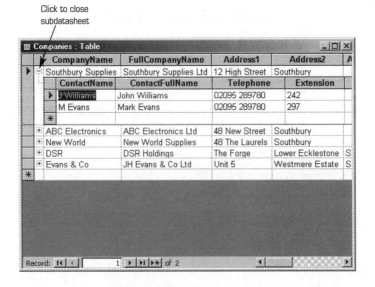

	CompanyName	FullCompanyName	Address1	Address2	A
⊟	Southbury Supplies	Southbury Supplies Ltd	12 High Street	Southbury	

	ContactName	ContactFullName	Telephone	Extension
▶	J Williams	John Williams	02095 289780	242
	M Evans	Mark Evans	02095 289780	297
*				

	CompanyName	FullCompanyName	Address1	Address2	A
⊞	ABC Electronics	ABC Electronics Ltd	48 New Street	Southbury	
⊞	New World	New World Supplies	48 The Laurels	Southbury	
⊞	DSR	DSR Holdings	The Forge	Lower Ecklestone	S
⊞	Evans & Co	JH Evans & Co Ltd	Unit 5	Westmere Estate	S
*					

Record: ◀◀ ◀ 1 ▶ ▶▶ ▶* of 2

3 The button is now shown as a ⊟ button. Click on this button
to close the subdatasheet again.

Insert a subdatasheet

RELATIONSHIPS

You can display a subdatasheet when a relationship has not been defined but two tables are linked in some way.

1 Display the first table in Datasheet view.

2 From the **Insert** menu, select **Subdatasheet**.

3 Click on the second table.

4 In the **Link Child Fields** box, click on the linked field from the second table.

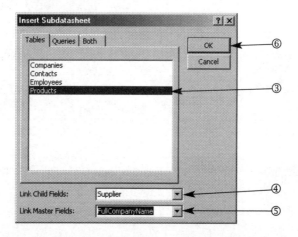

5 In the **Link Master Fields** box, click on the linked field from the first table.

6 Click on **OK**.

7 You are given the opportunity to create a relationship between the fields. Click on **Yes** if you want to do so.

8 Click on the ⊞ button to see the related records. The button changes to a ⊟ button.

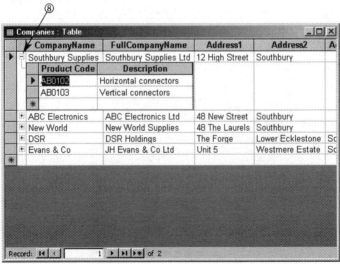

Enforce referential integrity

If there is a relationship between two tables then a change in one should normally result in a corresponding change in the other. For example, if one table contains product information and another contains additional information for each product, then deleting the record for a particular product should also result in the additional records being deleted. This process is called *referential integrity*.

1 In the database window, click on the ⬚ button.

2 Double-click on the link for which you want to enforce referential integrity.

3 Click on the check boxes to determine the type of referential integrity to be enforced.

4 Click on **OK**.

When the **Enforce Referential Integrity** box is turned on, you can select either or both of the following options:

• **Cascade Update Related Fields**: Changes to the linked field in the first table are automatically copied to the related field.

• **Cascade Delete Related Records**: Deleting a record in the

There are occasions when you do not want to enforce referential integrity. For example, if you delete the record for a department you do not want to delete the records for all employees assigned to that department. Instead, you should edit all the employee records to replace references to the department.

Database Queries

Create a query using the Query Wizard

A query allows you to retrieve information from your database. This can be a simple list of records or a more complex query where records are selected only if certain criteria are met.

Although you can create a query from scratch in Design view, it is easier to start by using the Query Wizard.

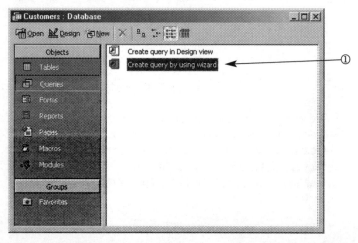

1 In the database window, click on the **Queries** object and double-click on **Create query by using wizard**.

2 In the **Tables/Queries** box, select the first table from which you want to extract records. Your query can combine records from more than one table, with the results showing a combination of data from both tables.

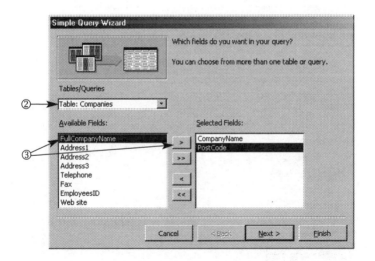

DATABASE QUERIES

3 Decide which fields you want to include in the results. Click on a field in the **Available Fields** list. Click on the top button to add the field to the **Selected Fields** list or the button below to add all fields. The other two buttons remove one or all fields from the selection.

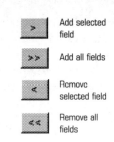

>	Add selected field
>>	Add all fields
<	Remove selected field
<<	Remove all fields

4 If required, select another table from the **Tables/Queries** box and add fields from the table to the **Selected Fields** list.

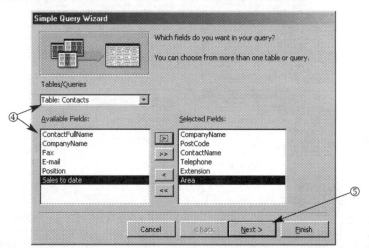

5 Repeat for other tables. Click on **Next** when the selection is complete.

6 If your query includes numeric or date/time fields, choose between showing detailed information for those fields or summaries of the data.

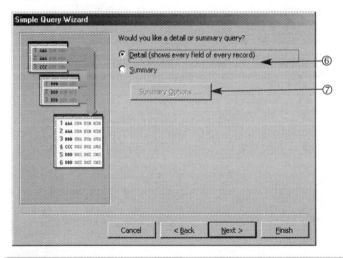

Any of the options you select in the wizard can be changed later in Design view.

7 If you choose the **Summary** option, you can decide which values to include. For each numeric and date/time field the query can calculate the total, average, minimum and maximum values, and produce a count of the records. Click on the boxes for the options you require and then click on **OK**.

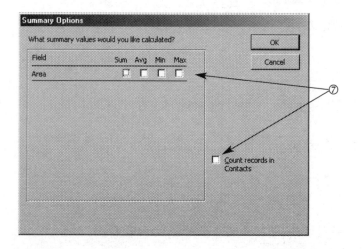

8 Type a name for the query and choose either to display the results of the query or open the query in Design view for editing. Click on **Finish**.

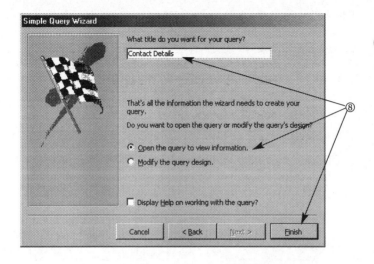

9 The results of the query are displayed. After viewing the results, close the query and click on **Yes** to save it.

Run a query

DATABASE QUERIES

To run a query:

1 In the database window, click on the **Queries** object.

2 Double-click on the query.

   OR

   Click on the query and then on the button.

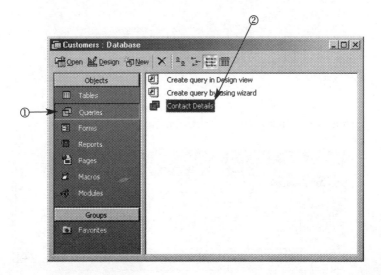

Edit a query

The queries you create are listed in the database window when the **Queries** object is selected. To view or edit a query:

1 In the database window, click on the **Queries** object.

2 Click on the query name on the right-hand side of the window.

3 Click on the ✎ Design button. The Design view is displayed, showing the tables in the query and how they are related.

4 Drag the bottom edge of the window so that you can see fields that are included in the query.

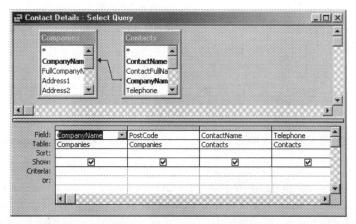

Create a query in Design view

1 In the database window, click on the **Queries** object and double-click on **Create query in Design view**.

2 The Design view is displayed, along with the Show Table dialog box. Select the first table from which you want to extract records and click on **Add**.

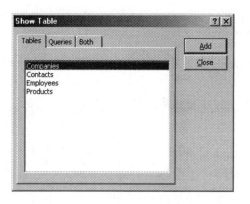

3 Repeat for other tables to be included in the query. Click on **Close**.

4 Insert the fields required for the query and add any necessary criteria (see pages 136 and 140).

Tables used in query

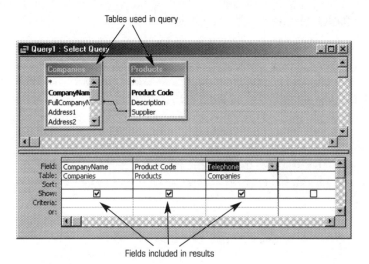

Fields included in results

5 Close the Design view and click on **Yes** to confirm that you want to save the query.

6 Type a name for the query and click on **OK**.

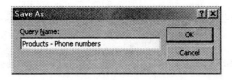

Add a field to a query

To add a field to a query:

1 Open the query in Design view.

2 Click on the **Field** box at the top of an empty column.

3 Click on the ▪ button and select a field from the drop-down list. The fields are listed in the form *table.field* and the list includes all fields in the tables shown in the top part of the view.

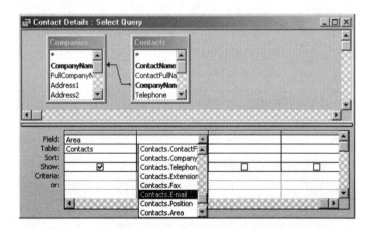

Change the order of fields in a query

To change the order of the fields as shown in Design view and in the results of the query:

1 In Design view, click at the top of the field to be moved, so that the whole column is highlighted.

2 Drag the column to its new position.

Drag pointer to new position

Click at top of field to select column

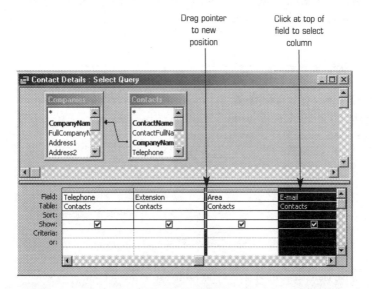

Hide a field

You can hide a field so that it does not appear in the query results. The field remains part of the query if it is used in the selection of records. In Design view:

• To hide a field, click on the **Show** check box in the field column, so that the check box is cleared.

• To show a field, click on the **Show** check box again, so that the check box is ticked.

Remove a field

To remove a field from the query (along with any selection criteria for that field):

1 In Design view, click at the top of the field to be deleted, so that the whole column is highlighted.

2 Press **[Delete]**.

   OR

   From the **Edit** menu, select **Delete Columns**.

The field and its data in the table are not affected.

Add fields from another table

You can expand a query to include fields from other tables in the database.

1 Open the query in Design view.

2 From the **Query** menu, select **Show Table**.

3 Click on the table name and then on **Add**.

4 Repeat for any other tables that are required. Click on **Close**.

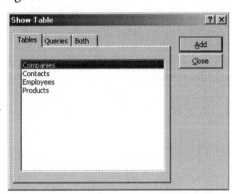

Remove a table from a query

A table can be removed from a query. All fields from that table will be removed.

1 Open the query in Design view.

2 Right-click on the table and select **Remove Table**.

Specify criteria for a field

You can reduce the number of records displayed by a query by specifying *criteria*. Records will only be displayed if the criteria are satisfied. For example, you can display all contacts with a particular area code or all employees in a selected department.

1 Open the query in Design view.

2 Click on the **Criteria** box for the required field and enter the value against which the records are to be tested.

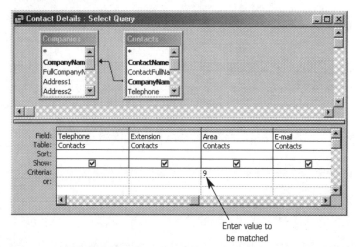

Enter value to
be matched

3 Close the Design view and save the changes.

4 Run the query. Only matching records are displayed.

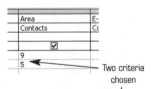

CompanyName	PostCode	ContactName	Telephone	Exte	Area Code
Southbury Supplies	SY12 4AQ	J Williams	02095 289780	242	9
Southbury Supplies	SY12 4AQ	M Evans	02095 289780	297	9
ABC Electronics	SY12 3QS	T Smith	02095 371206		9

Contact Details : Select Query

Record: 1 ▶ ▶| ▶* of 3

Matching values

Specify multiple criteria for a field

You can broaden the query by
specifying a value in the **or** box,
immediately below the **Criteria** value.
The query now lists records that
match either of the specified values.

Area	E-
Contacts	Co
☑	
9	
5	

Two criteria
chosen

Contact Details : Select Query

CompanyName	PostCode	ContactName	Telephone	Exte	Area Code
Southbury Supplies	SY12 4AQ	J Williams	02095 289780	242	9
Southbury Supplies	SY12 4AQ	M Evans	02095 289780	297	9
ABC Electronics	SY12 3QS	T Smith	02095 371206		9
Evans & Co	SY11 2NG	J K Evans	07908 206989		5

Record: 1 ▶ ▶| ▶* of 4

Specify criteria for several fields

You can further refine your query by specifying criteria for more than one field.

1 Open the query in Design view.

2 For each field, click on the **Criteria** box and enter the value against which the records are to be tested.

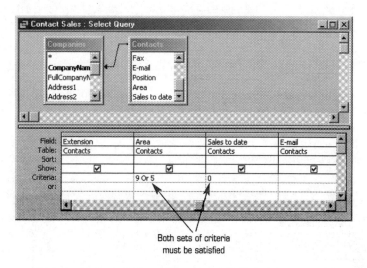

Both sets of criteria must be satisfied

3 Close the Design view and save the changes.

4 Run the query.

CompanyName	ContactName	Telephone	Exte	Area Code	Sales to date
Southbury Supplies	J Williams	02095 289780	242	9	£0.00
ABC Electronics	T Smith	02095 371206		9	£0.00
Evans & Co	J K Evans	07908 206989		5	£0.00

Record: 1 ▶ ▶I ▶* of 3

The results of the query depend on where the criteria are entered:

Records for which Area Code is 9 or 5 AND Sales to date is 0

• If the criteria are entered on the same row, all criteria must be satisfied for the record to be included.

• If the criteria are entered on different rows, records are included if any of the criteria is satisfied.

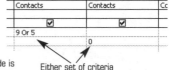

Area	Sales to date	E-
Contacts	Contacts	Co
☑	☑	
9 Or 5		
	0	

Records for which Area Code is 9 or 5 OR Sales to date is 0

Either set of criteria must be satisfied

CompanyName	ContactName	Telephone	Ext	Area Code	Sales to date
Southbury Supplies	J Williams	02095 289780	242	9	£0.00
Southbury Supplies	M Evans	02095 289780	297	9	£100.00
DSR	N James	02095 650737		2	£0.00
ABC Electronics	T Smith	02095 371206		9	£0.00
Evans & Co	J K Evans	07908 206989		5	£0.00

Record: 1 ▶ ▶I ▶* of 5

Sort records in a query

The results of a query can be sorted according to the contents of one or more fields.

1 Open the query in Design view.

2 For each field to be sorted, click on the **Sorted** box, click on the ▾ button and choose either **Ascending** or **Descending**. If the sort is based on more than one field, the values are sorted from left to right (so you may need to change the order of the columns).

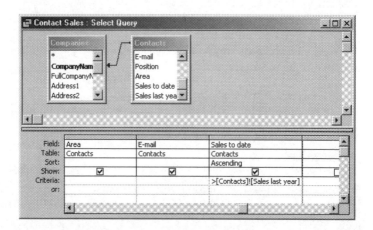

3 Close the Design view and save the changes.

4 Run the query. The records are sorted.

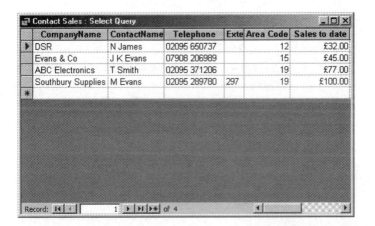

CompanyName	ContactName	Telephone	Exte	Area Code	Sales to date
DSR	N James	02095 650737		12	£32.00
Evans & Co	J K Evans	07908 206989		15	£45.00
ABC Electronics	T Smith	02095 371206		19	£77.00
Southbury Supplies	M Evans	02095 289780	297	19	£100.00

Record: 1 ▶ ▶I ▶* of 4

Cancel a sort

To cancel the sorting of a particular field, click on the ▼ button in the **Sorted** box and choose '**(not sorted)**'.

Advanced Queries

Use the Expression Builder

The criteria described in the previous chapter provide for very simple record matching, with field contents being compared against constant values. You can use the Expression Builder to create much more sophisticated criteria.

1 Open the query in Design view.

2 Click on the **Criteria** box for the required field.

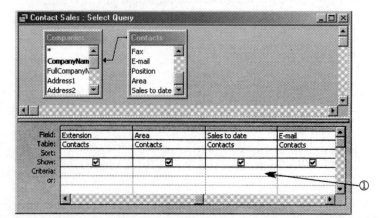

3 Click on the 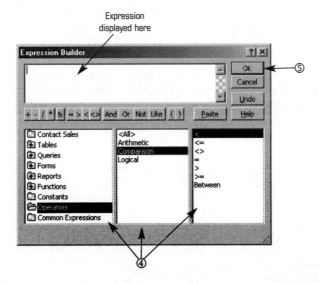 button on the Access toolbar. The Expression Builder is displayed.

Expression displayed here

4 Use the operators to build an expression against which the field contents will be tested. When you are familiar with the Expression Builder, you can type expressions directly into the box at the top.

5 Click on **OK**.

Compare values in criteria

The criteria for a query can compare a field value against another field or a constant value, rather than simply look for specific values. For example, you may want to find sales values greater than £100.

1 In the Expression Builder, click on **Operators** in the left-hand box, **Comparison** in the middle box and an operator in the right-hand box.

2 Click on the **Paste** button.

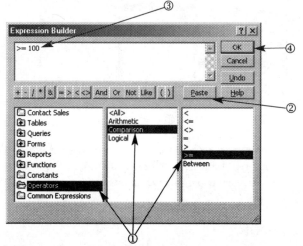

3 Type the value against which the comparison is to be made.

4 Click on **OK**.

You can use the following comparison operators:

=	Equal
<>	Not equal
<	Less than
<=	Less or equal
>	Greater than
>=	Greater or equal

In addition, the **Between** operator checks that the field lies between two specified values. Replace the two occurrences of '<<Expr>>' with the values against which the field is to be checked.

tip

If the required operator is =, <, > or <>, you can add it to the expression by clicking on the appropriate button in the middle of the Expression Builder.

Combine expressions in criteria

You can combine two expressions to form a more complex expression. For example, you may want to find sales values that are greater than one value but not equal to another value.

1 In the Expression Builder, enter the first expression.

2 Click on **Operators** in the left-hand box, **Logical** in the middle box and an operator in the right-hand box.

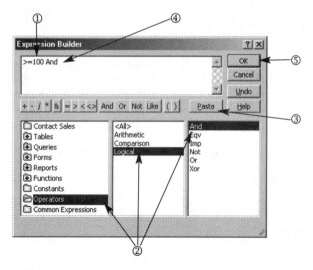

3 Click on the **Paste** button.

4 Enter the second expression.

5 Click on **OK**.

You can use the following logical operators:

And Both expressions must be true for the combined expression to be true.

Eqv Both expressions must be true or both must be false (equivalence).

Imp Either the first expression must be false or the second expression must be false.

Not Negates the expression.

Or One (or both) of the expressions must be true.

Xor One of the expressions must be true but not both (exclusive or).

If you use the Not operator, it must be placed in front of a single expression. The other operators must be be placed between two expressions.

Use another field in an expression

The criteria for a field can be based on the value of another field (either a field in the same record or a field from a related table).

1 In the Expression Builder, select the comparison operator.

2 Double-click to the left of **Tables** in the left-hand box, so that the tables are listed. Click on the required table.

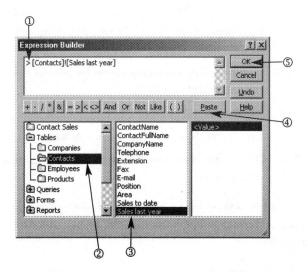

3 Click on the required field in the middle box.

4 Click on the **Paste** button.

5 Click on **OK**.

The reference to the field appears in the form:

[*table*]![*field*]

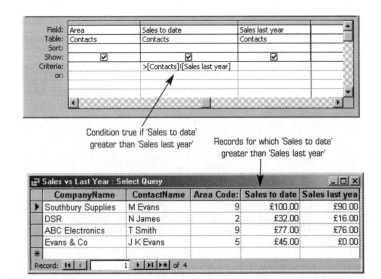

Condition true if 'Sales to date'
greater than 'Sales last year'

Records for which 'Sales to date'
greater than 'Sales last year'

Use functions in an expression

Access includes a number of built-in functions for performing specific tasks within an expression. These can be included in the expression in a similar way to field references:

1 In the Expression Builder, click to the left of **Functions** in the left-hand box, so that the functions are listed.

2 Click on **Built-In Functions**.

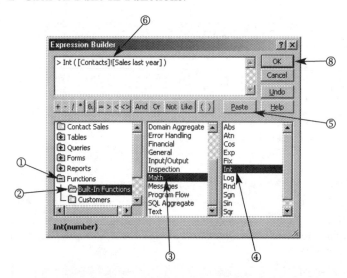

3 Click on one of the categories of built-in functions in the middle box.

4 Click on a function in the right-hand box.

5 Click on the **Paste** button.

6 Replace '<<number>>' in the brackets with the value to be used by the function.

7 Complete the expression.

8 Click on **OK**.

The brackets following a function can include a constant value, the value from another field or an expression. For example:

>Int([Contacts]![Sales last year])

This criterion is satisfied if the field being tested has a value greater than the integer part of the value held for the field 'Sales last year'.

You can make the expressions as complicated as you like. For example, the brackets after a function can include further function calls.

Calculate a field in a query

While a query is running, you can generate an additional field for which the value is calculated by the query.

1 Open the query in Design view and click on the **Field** box in an empty column.

2 Click on the button on the Access toolbar.

3 In the Expression Builder, create an expression that will perform the calculation.

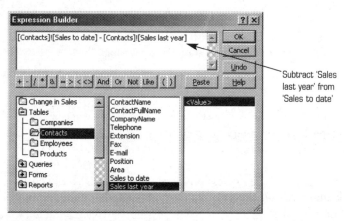

Subtract 'Sales last year' from 'Sales to date'

4 Click on **OK**. The expression is shown in the **Field** box.

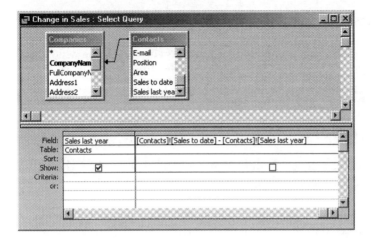

5 Close and save the query.

6 In the database window, double-click on the query to run it. The new field (named Expr1) is added to the results window.

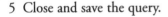

CompanyNam	ContactName	Area	Sales to date	Sales last year	Expr1
ABC Electronic	T Smith	9	£77.00	£76.00	£1.00
DSR	N James	2	£32.00	£16.00	£16.00
Evans & Co	J K Evans	5	£45.00	£0.00	£45.00
New World	R Fletcher	4	£50.00	£75.00	-£25.00
Southbury Supr	J Williams	9	£59.00	£124.00	-£65.00
Southbury Supr	M Evans	9	£100.00	£90.00	£10.00

Record: 1 of 6

You can define a query that prompts you for a value while the query is running. This *parameter* value can be used in an expression, so you can control the way in which the results are derived. For example, you may want to return all records for which a particular field is above a given value, with this value specified when the query is run.

1 Open the query in Design view and click on the **Criteria** box for the required field.

2 Enter the expression to be tested. The parameter should be included in the expression in square brackets. You can use any text you like to describe the parameter. If necessary, use the

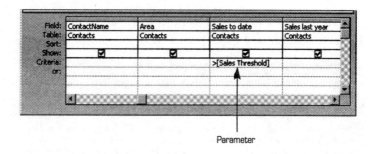

Parameter

Expression Builder to help construct the expression, typing in the parameter at the appropriate point.

3 Close and save the query.

4 In the database window, double-click on the query to run it.

5 The Enter Parameter Value dialog box is displayed, prompting you for a value for the parameter. The text in the dialog box is the text that was given in square brackets. Enter a value and click on **OK**.

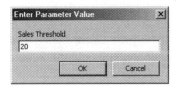

6 The results window is displayed.

Each time you run the query you can give a different value for the parameter and get a different set of results.

CompanyName	ContactName	Area Cod	Sales to date	Sales last year
Southbury Supplies	J Williams	9	£59.00	£124.00
Southbury Supplies	M Evans	9	£100.00	£90.00
New World	R Fletcher	4	£50.00	£75.00
DSR	N James	2	£32.00	£16.00
ABC Electronics	T Smith	9	£77.00	£76.00
Evans & Co	J K Evans	5	£45.00	£0.00

Sales Above Threshold : Select Query

Record: 1 of 6

The join type determines the number of records that are displayed in the query.

1 Click on the ⊞ button.

2 Double-click on the relationship link.

3 Click on **Join Type**.

4 Click on one of the join options and click on **OK**.

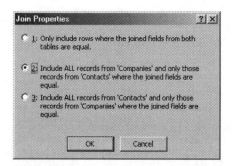

5 Click on **OK** in the Edit Relationships dialog box.

6 Close the Relationships window.

The join type is one of the following:

• A row is included in the results only when the joined fields are the same in both tables.

• A row is included in the results for all records in the first table, even when there is no matching record in the second table.

• A row is included in the results for all records in the second table, even when there is no matching record in the first table.

If you choose either of the last two options, some fields in the results table may be blank.

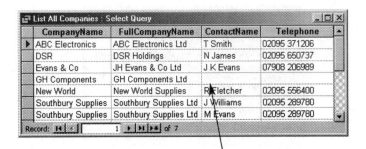

When join type is 2, record is included even
if no matching record in second table

Query Wizards

Find duplicate records

You can produce a list of records that have duplicate values in a particular field. For example, you can produce a list of companies for which there are multiple contacts.

1 In the database window, click on the **Queries** object.

2 Click on the New button.

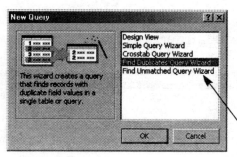

Options for creating new queries

3 Click on **Find Duplicates Query Wizard** and click on **OK**.

4 Click on the table in which you want to search for duplicate
fields and click on **Next**.

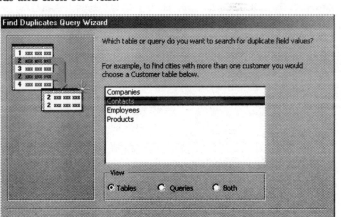

The field containing duplicates can be any field in the table; it
does not necessarily have to be a key field. You can search in
more than one field at a time.

5 Select the fields that may contain duplicate information. Use the buttons in the middle of the dialog box to add fields to the selection or remove selected fields. You can select as many fields as you like from the table. Click on **Next**.

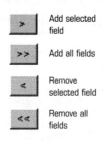

>	Add selected field
>>	Add all fields
<	Remove selected field
<<	Remove all fields

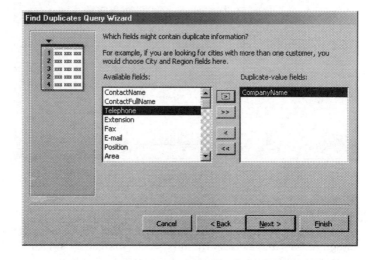

Find Duplicates Query Wizard

Which fields might contain duplicate information?

For example, if you are looking for cities with more than one customer, you would choose City and Region fields here.

Available fields:

ContactName
ContactFullName
Telephone
Extension
Fax
E-mail
Position
Area

Duplicate-value fields:

CompanyName

Cancel   < Back   Next >   Finish

6 Choose any other fields you want to appear in the query for those records that have duplicate values. Again, use the keys in the middle of the dialog box to add fields to the selection or remove fields from the selection. Click on **Next** when the selection is complete.

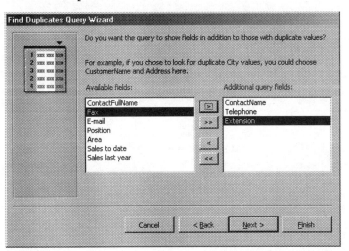

tip

At any stage you can click on Back to go back to the previous stage; Finish to complete the query with the remaining defaults; or Cancel to abandon the query.

QUERY WIZARDS

7 Type a name for the query, choose whether to view or edit the query, and click on **Finish**.

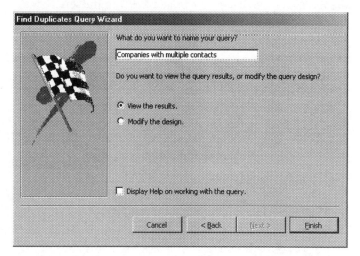

The results of the query are displayed.

Records for companies with multiple contacts

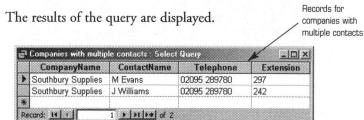

Find unmatched records

You can produce a list of records from one table for which there are no corresponding records in a related table. For example, you can produce a list of companies for which there are no contacts.

1 In the database window, click on the **Queries** object.

2 Click on the 🔲 New button.

3 Click on **Find Unmatched Query Wizard** and click on **OK**.

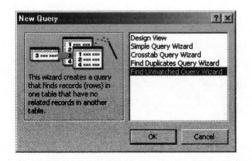

4 Click on the table that may have no matching records; for example, click on the Companies table if you are looking for companies with no contacts. Click on **Next**.

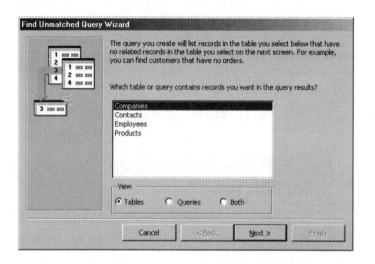

5 Click on the related table (which may not contain any records corresponding to those in the first table). For example, if the first table was Companies, the second may be Contacts. Click on **Next**.

6 Identify the fields that link the two tables together. Click on the linking field in each table and then click on the <=> button. Click on **Next**.

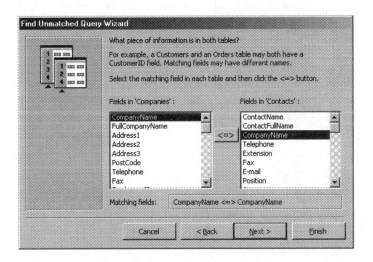

7 Choose the fields you want to appear in the query for those records that have no matches. Use the keys in the middle of the dialog box to add fields to the selection or remove fields from the selection. Click on **Next** when the selection is complete.

QUERY WIZARDS

8 Type a name for the query, choose whether to view or edit the query, and click on **Finish**.

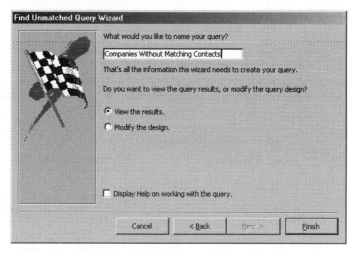

The results of the query are displayed.

Create a crosstab query

A crosstab query summarizes numeric values in a table. For example, you can display the sales values by area and company, with totals for each area.

1 In the database window, click on the **Queries** object.

2 Click on the 🔲 New button.

3 Click on **Find Duplicates Query Wizard** and click on **OK**.

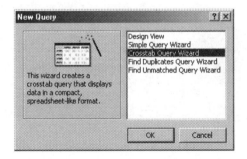

4 Click on the table for which you want to produce the summary. Click on **Next**.

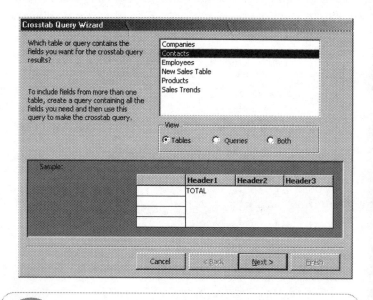

tip

You can also produce a crosstab query based on another query. This is useful where a query has been used to create numeric fields.

5 Select the field whose values are to be shown in the row headings on the left-hand side of the results table. Use the buttons in the middle of the dialog box to add fields to the selection or remove selected fields. You can select up to three fields. Click on **Next**.

Click on field   Click to select field

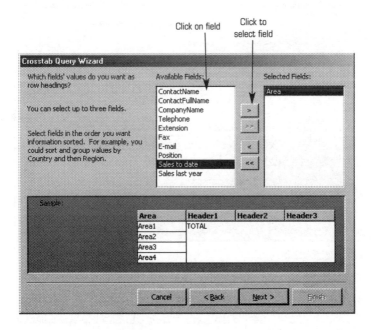

6 Select the field whose values are to be shown along the top of the results table. Only one field can be selected here. Click on **Next**.

```
Crosstab Query Wizard

Which field's values do you want as        ContactName
column headings?                           ContactFullName
                                           CompanyName
                                           Telephone
For example, you would select              Extension
Employee Name to see each                  Fax
employee's name as a column heading.       E-mail
                                           Position
                                           Sales to date
                                           Sales last year
```

Sample:			
Area	**CompanyNan**	**CompanyNan**	**CompanyNan**
Area1	TOTAL		
Area2			
Area3			
Area4			

```
              Cancel      < Back      Next >      Finish
```

tip

Deciding which fields to use can be a problem until you have produced the query. Remember that you can always delete a query after running it and start again.

7 Select the field whose values are to be summarized in the main body of the table. Select the function that is to be calculated (for example, **Sum** for a total of matching values or **Avg** to calculate an average). Decide whether or not to include a total of the displayed values for each row. Click on **Next**.

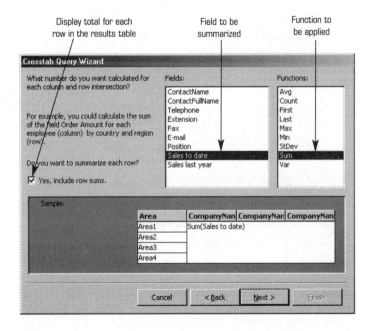

8 Type a name for the query, choose whether to view or edit the query, and click on **Finish**.

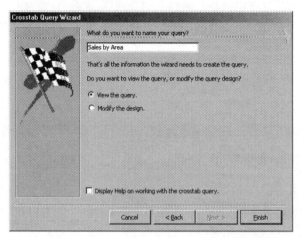

The results of the query are displayed. After closing the results window you can re-run the query at any time.

Area Code:	Total Of Sales	ABC Electronic	DSR	Evans & Co	New World
12	£32.00		£32.00		
14	£50.00				£50.0
15	£45.00			£45.00	
19	£236.00	£77.00			
99	£0.00				

Record: 14 ◀ | 1 ▶ ▶I ▶* of 5

Edit a wizard query

You can edit any query that has been generated by a wizard.

1 In the database window, click on the **Queries** object.

2 Click on the query and then on the ![Design] button.

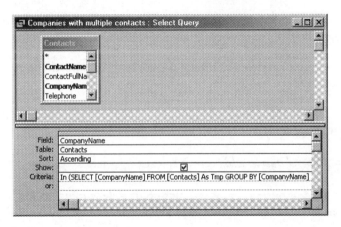

3 Make the changes to the query design.

4 Close the Design view and save the changes.

Query Operations

Create different types of query

Access allows you to create several different types of query:

• *Select queries* select records according to specified criteria (see page 126).

• *Crosstab queries* summarize the contents of numeric fields (see page 171).

• *Make-table queries* generate new tables from the query results (see page 179).

• *Append queries* add records to existing queries (see page 183).

• *Update queries* change existing records depending on the results of the queries (see page 189).

• *Delete queries* delete records in existing tables (see page 186).

You can change any query into a query of another type by opening the query in Design view and selecting from the **Query** menu.

Make a new table from a query

The table that is produced when you run a query is a temporary table; the layout is stored but no extra data is held. In particular, the data created for calculated fields exists only as long as the query results window is open.

You can create a permanent table from the results produced by a query.

1 Open an existing query in Design view or create a new query.

2 Click on the  button on the toolbar and select **Make-Table Query** from the drop-down list.

   OR

   From the **Query** menu, select **Make-Table Query**.

3 Type a name for the new table or, if you want to replace an existing table, select the table from the drop-down list. The new table can be stored in either the current database or another database (in which case you must specify the filename). Click on **OK**.

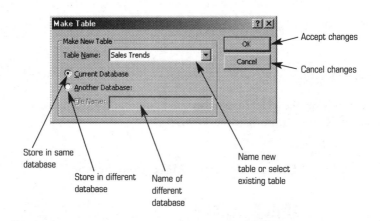

Accept changes

Cancel changes

Store in same database

Store in different database

Name of different database

Name new table or select existing table

tip

This process modifies an existing query, rather than creating a new one. Therefore you may wish to make a copy of the query before you start.

4 Close the query in Design view and save the changes. The query is identified by a different icon in the database window.

5 Double-click on the query to run it.

6 A warning message is displayed. Click on **Yes** to create the new table (any previous version of the same table is replaced).

7 A further warning message tells you how many records the new table will have. Click on **Yes**.

8 The table is created. To view the table, click on the **Tables** object in the database window and then double-click on the table name.

CompanyName	ContactName	Area	Sales to da	Sales last y	Expr1
Southbury Supplies	J Williams	9	£59.00	£124.00	-£65.00
Southbury Supplies	M Evans	9	£100.00	£90.00	£10.00
New World	R Fletcher	4	£50.00	£75.00	-£25.00
DSR	N James	2	£32.00	£16.00	£16.00
ABC Electronics	T Smith	9	£77.00	£76.00	£1.00
Evans & Co	J K Evans	5	£45.00	£0.00	£45.00

Sales Trends : Table

Record: 1 of 6

You can treat this new table like any other table. However, remember that it will be replaced when you next run the query and any changes you make will then be lost.

Add records to a table using a query

The results from a query can be added to an existing table as new records. The query must include the primary key for the table (if there is one).

1 Open an existing query in Design view or create a new query.

2 Click on the button on the toolbar and select **Append Query** from the drop-down list.

> **OR**

From the **Query** menu, select **Append Query**.

3 Select the table from the drop-down list. The new table can be stored in either the current database or another database (in which case you must specify the filename). Click on **OK**.

4 Close the query in Design view and save the changes. The query is identified by a different icon in the database window.

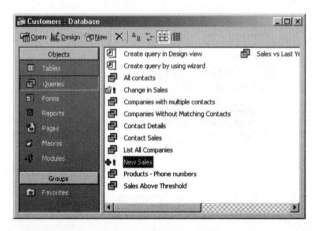

5 Double-click on the query to run it.

6 A warning message is displayed. Click on **Yes** to update the table by adding records to it.

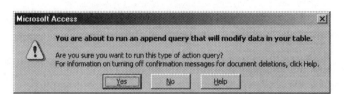

7 A further warning message tells you how many records the new table will have. Click on **Yes**.

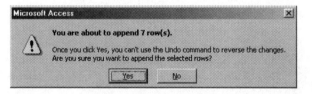

8 The table is updated. To view the table, click on the **Tables** object in the database window and then double-click on the table name.

If the table has a primary key and the appended records would be duplicates, the new records are not added.

Delete records using a query

A query can be used to delete all records that satisfy given criteria.

1 In the database window, click on the **Queries** object and double-click on **Create query in Design view**.

2 The Design view is displayed, along with the Show Table dialog box. Select the table from which you want to delete records and click on **Add**. Click on **Close**.

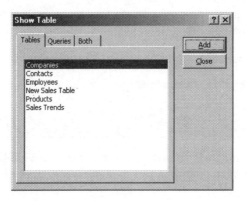

3 Insert the fields required for the query and add any necessary criteria to select records to be deleted (see pages 136 and 140).

4 Click on the 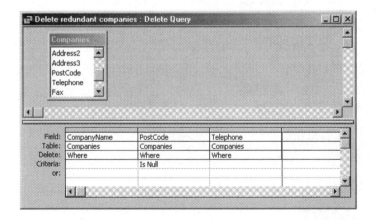 button on the toolbar and select **Delete Query** from the drop-down list.

OR

From the **Query** menu, select **Delete Query**.

5 The Design view now shows that the query contains delete criteria. Close the Design view and click on **Yes** to confirm that you want to save the query. Give the query a name.

Delete redundant companies : Delete Query

Companies
Address2
Address3
PostCode
Telephone
Fax

Field:	CompanyName	PostCode	Telephone	
Table:	Companies	Companies	Companies	
Delete:	Where	Where	Where	
Criteria:		Is Null		
or:				

5 Double-click on the query to run it.

6 A warning message is displayed. Click on **Yes** to update the table by deleting matching records.

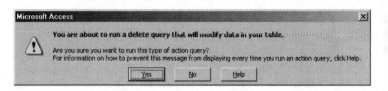

7 A further warning message tells you how many records will be deleted. Click on **Yes**.

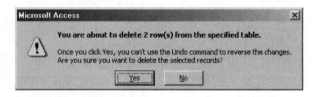

8 The table is updated and can be viewed.

tip

Before converting your query to a Delete query, make a copy of it and rename the copy. You can run the copy query first to see which records will be removed by the Delete query.

Update records using a query

A query can be used to update all records that satisfy given criteria by performing some operations on existing values in the table. For example, you might run a query to set certain fields to zero at the start of a year.

1 In the database window, click on the **Queries** object and double-click on **Create query in Design view**.

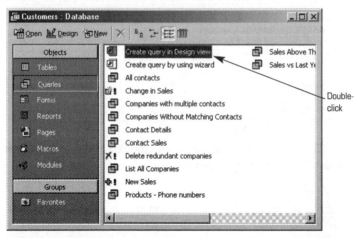

2 The Design view is displayed, along with the Show Table dialog box. Select the table that is to be updated and click on **Add**. Click on **Close**.

3 Insert the fields required for the query and add any necessary criteria to select the records to be updated (see pages 136 and 140).

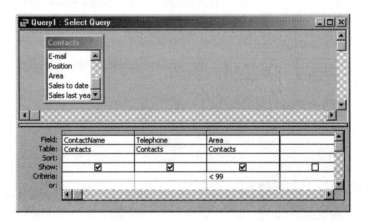

4 Click on the [≡]▼ button on the toolbar and select **Update Query** from the drop-down list.

OR

From the **Query** menu, select **Update Query**.

5 Click on the **Update To** box for the field that is to be updated.

6 Click on the 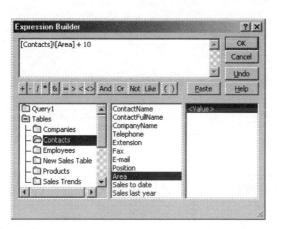 button on the Access toolbar to display the Expression Builder. Enter an expression to calculate the new value for the field. Click on **OK**.

tip

The expression can include constant values, the values of other fields or the value of the same field. If you use the same field, you will only be able to run the query once.

7 The Design view now shows the update expression. Close the Design view and click on **Yes** to confirm that you want to save the query.

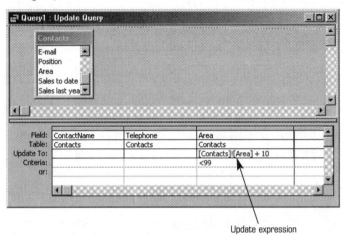

Field:	ContactName	Telephone	Area	
Table:	Contacts	Contacts	Contacts	
Update To:			[Contacts]![Area] + 10	
Criteria:			<99	
or:				

Update expression

5 Double-click on the query to run it.

6 A warning message is displayed. Click on **Yes** to update the table.

7 A further warning message tells you how many records will be updated. Click on **Yes**.

8 The table is updated and can be viewed.

Filter a table

As an alternative to a query, you can temporarily reduce the
number of records being displayed by running a filter. For
example, you can filter a table to produce a list of records that
have a particular value in a field.

1 Open the table in Datasheet view.

2 Right-click on the field whose value is to be used for the filter.

3 Select **Filter by Selection** to list only records with that value
in the field.

Other filter options

You can refine an existing filter:

• Right-click on a value in another field and select **Filter by Selection** to reduce the current set of records to those with that value.

• Right-click an another field and type a value into the **Filter For** box. This reduces the set of records to those with the specified value.

• Right-click on a value in another field and select **Filter Excluding Selection** to list records that do *not* have the selected value.

Remove a filter

When a table is being filtered, a FLTR symbol is displayed in the status bar.

To remove the filter, right-click on the table and select **Remove Filter/Sort**.

Filter by form

You can set up complicated filters using the **Filter By Form** option.

1 Open the table in Datasheet view.

2 From the **Records** menu, select **Filter** and **Filter By Form**.

3 For each field to be included in the filter, click on the blank box and select the value for the filter.

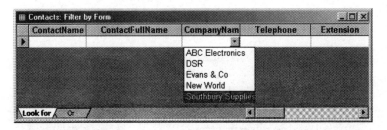

4 From the **Filter** menu, select **Apply Filter/Sort**.

The filtered table will show only those records for which the values in the filter fields all match the filter values.

Specify alternative values for a filter

The filters described above result in records being displayed only if they match all filter values. You can also specify alternative values for a field.

1 Open the table in Datasheet view. From the **Records** menu, select **Filter** and **Filter By Form**.

2 For each field to be included in the filter, click on the blank box and select the value for the filter.

3 For the alternative set of values, click on the **Or** tab at the bottom of the window and then select values for one or more fields. Repeat with additional **Or** tabs if required.

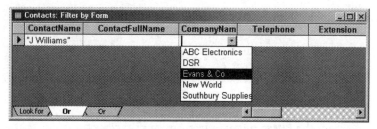

4 From the **Filter** menu, select **Apply Filter/Sort**.

The filtered table will show records that match any of the groups of filter values.

Save a filter as a query

When you have applied a filter to a table, you can keep the filter for future use by saving it as a query.

1 Set up the filter on the table in Datasheet view.

2 From the **Records** menu, select **Filter** and **Advanced Filter/Sort**. The filter is opened in Design view.

3 From the **File** menu, select **Save As Query**.

4 Type a name for the query and click on **OK**.

5 Close the filter in Design view.

6 Close the table in Datasheet view, without saving the changes.

You can now run the new query.

Change the margins

The **Margins** tab on the Page Setup dialog box changes the space around the outside of the printout.

1 Open a table in Datasheet view or run a query.

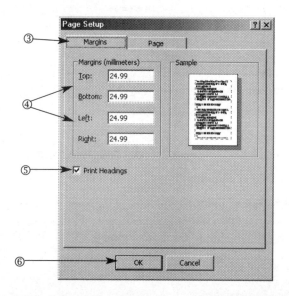

2 From the **File** menu, select **Page Setup**.

3 Click on the **Margins** tab.

4 Enter the size of the top, bottom, left and right margins. The top and bottom margins include the space used by the header and footer respectively.

5 By default, the top margin of each page includes a header that contains the table or query name and the current date; the bottom margin includes the page number. If you do not want this information printed, clear the **Print Headings** check box.

6 Click on **OK**.

tip

For more control over the printing options, either create a report in Access (see page 206) or export the data to some other program, such as Word (see page 236).

Change the page size and layout

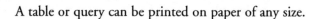

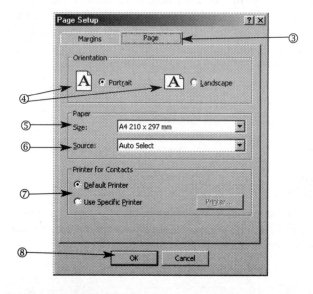

A table or query can be printed on paper of any size.

1 Open a table in Datasheet view or run a query.

2 From the **File** menu, select **Page Setup**.

3 Click on the **Page** tab.

4 Select either **Portrait** (tall, thin) or **Landscape** (short, wide).

Choose the required paper **Size** from the drop-down list.

For printers with multiple paper trays, select the tray from the **Source** drop-down list.

Choose either the default Windows printer or another printer. If you select the option for another printer, you must click on the **Printer** button and choose a printer from the list. You can also change the properties for the selected printer.

PRINTING

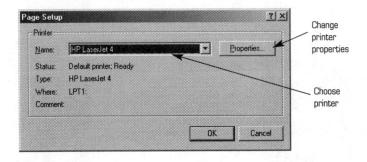

Change printer properties

Choose printer

Click on **OK**.

Preview the pages to print

Click on the 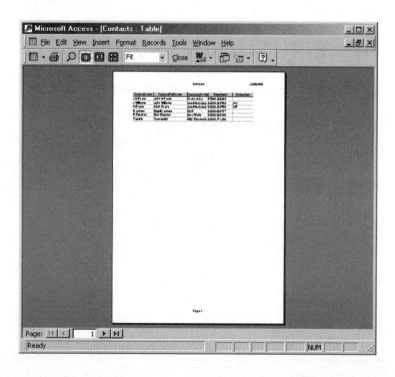 button to see what the table or query will look like when it is printed. Alternatively, select **Print Preview** from the **File** menu.

The buttons at the top of the Print Preview window are used as follows:

- Click on to start the print process.

- Click on 🔍 to magnify the preview or show the whole page at once.

- Click on 🔳 to display one page in the window.

- Click on 🔳🔳 to display two pages side by side.

- Click on 🔳🔳 to display some other combination of multiple pages.

- Click on `Fit      ▾` to choose the magnification or make the display fit the window.

- Click on `Close` to return to normal Datasheet view.

- Click on 🔃 to display help on the Print Preview window.

The other buttons take you to different windows.

Click on the buttons at the bottom of the window to go to the next or previous page, or the first or last page.

Print a table or query

To print the table or query (or just the selected records):

1 From the **File** menu, select **Print**.

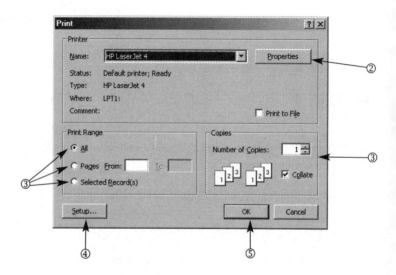

2 Click on the **Properties** button if you want to change the way the printer is set up.

3 Change any of the print defaults, as required (see below).

4 Click on the **Setup** button if you want to change the margins (see page 198).

5 Click on **OK**.

You can change the way the sheets are printed as follows:

• In the **Print Range** section, choose what is to be printed. Click on **All** to print everything; click on **Pages** to print only selected pages and enter the first and last page numbers to print; or click on **Selected Record(s)** to print the records currently selected in the table.

• In the **Copies** section, specify the number of copies to print. For multiple copies, click on **Collate** if you want to print the copies as complete sets (rather than printing multiple copies of each page in turn).

tip

Click on the button to start the print process without displaying the Print dialog box. (This will print with all the default settings.)

Creating Reports

Create a report with one record per page

The easiest way to create a report is to use the AutoReport
Wizard. This has options for creating two types of report.

To create a report with one record printed on each page:

1 In the database window, click on the **Reports** object.

2 Click on the ⊞ New button.

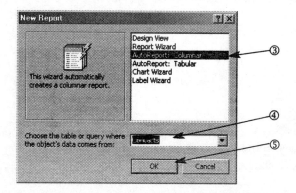

3 Click on **AutoReport: Columnar**.

4 Select a table or query in the drop-down box at the bottom of the New Report dialog box.

5 Click on **OK**.

The report is
generated and
can be printed
by selecting
Print from the
File menu.

You can view
the report using
the Print
Preview options
(see page 202).

Close the report
by clicking on
the ✕ button.
You are given
the opportunity
to save the
report.

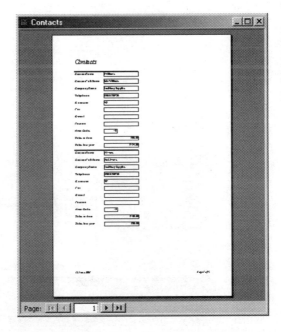

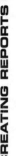

Create a tabular report

To create a tabular report, with one record for each row of the printout:

1 In the database window, click on the **Reports** object.

2 Click on the 🗗New button.

3 Click on **AutoReport: Tabular**.

4 Select a table or query in the drop-down box at the bottom of the New Report dialog box.

5 Click on **OK**.

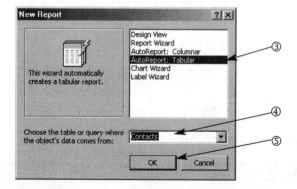

The report is generated and can be printed by selecting **Print** from the **File** menu.

You can view the report using the Print Preview options (see page 202).

Close the report by clicking on the button. You are given the opportunity to save the report. Saved reports are stored as Report objects in the database window.

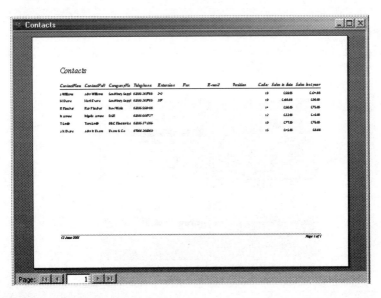

Create a report using the Report Wizard

For more control over a report than is offered by the AutoReport Wizard, use the Report Wizard.

1 In the database window, click on the **Reports** object.

2 Click on the ⊞New button.

3 Click on **Report Wizard**.

4 Select a table or query in the drop-down box at the bottom of the New Report dialog box.

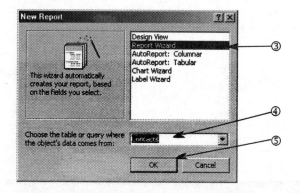

5 Click on **OK**.

6 Choose the fields to be shown on
the report using the buttons in the
middle of the dialog box. Click on
the top button to add the field to the
report or the button below to add all
fields. The other two buttons remove
one or all fields from the report.
Repeat this process with other tables
and fields, if required. Click on **Next**.

>	Add selected field
>>	Add all fields
<	Remove selected field
<<	Remove all fields

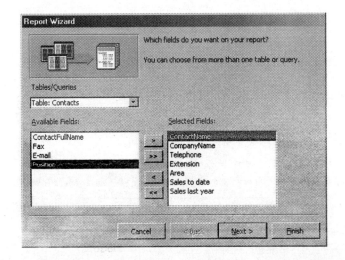

7 If you want to group records in any way, select one or more fields by which they will be grouped. The records will be sorted according to the values in the selected fields. To change the way the groupings are applied, click on **Grouping Options**. After setting the options, click on **Next**.

Add grouping level
for selected field

Group by
company name

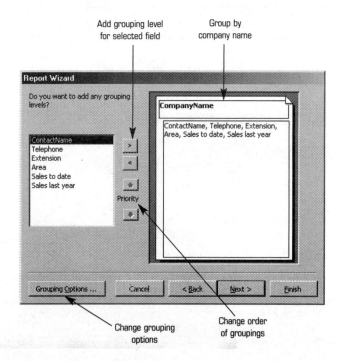

Change grouping
options

Change order
of groupings

8 Choose the field by which each block of detail records is to be sorted. You can select up to four fields for sorting and each one can be in either ascending or descending order. You can also specify whether you want summary information to be printed for numeric fields. After setting the options, click on **Next**.

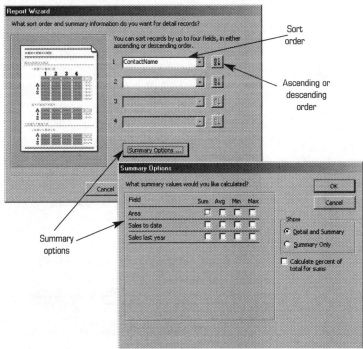

9 Choose a layout for the report. Click on **Next**.

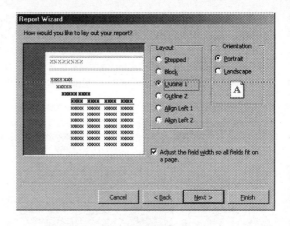

10 Choose the style for the text in the report. Click on **Next**.

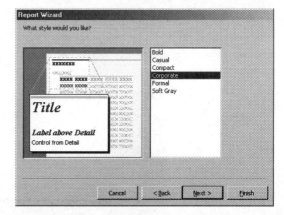

11 Type a name for the report, choose whether to view or edit the report, and click on **Finish**.

The report is generated and can be printed by selecting **Print** from the **File** menu.

You can view the report using the Print Preview options (see page 202).

Close the report by clicking on the button. The report is stored as a Report object in the database window.

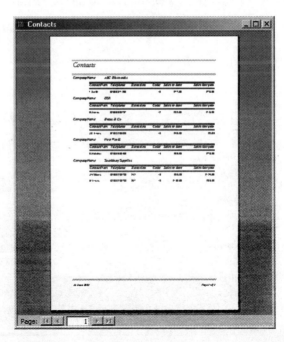

Edit a report

In Design view, you can edit a report that has been created by a wizard. You can also use Design view for creating reports from scratch.

1 In the database window, click on the **Reports** object.

2 Click on the report and then on the 🔍 Design button.

3 Make the changes to the report design.

4 Close the Design view and save the changes.

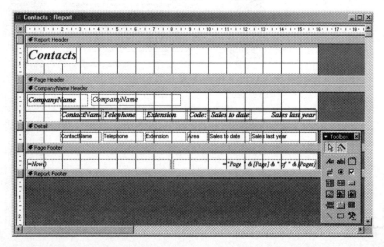

Change a report in Design view

In Design view, you can create or rearrange a report:

• Double-click on a report section to see a list of properties for that section. The dialog box has a number of tabs, with properties for different aspects of the section. Different sections have different lists of properties, any of which can be changed.

Section: ReportHeader	
Format	Data	Event	Other	**All**
Name	ReportHeader
Force New Page	None
New Row Or Col	None
Keep Together	Yes
Visible	Yes
Can Grow	No
Can Shrink	No
Height	1.679cm
Back Color	16777215
Special Effect	Flat
Tag	
On Format	
On Print	

• The Toolbox contains a number of controls, which help organize your report and improve its appearance. Click on a control on the Toolbox and then click on the report to add a control. Right-click on the control and select **Properties** to change the way a particular control works.

• From the **View** menu, select **Field List** to display the fields for the table. Drag additional fields onto the report.

Creating Forms

Create a form for entering a single record

Forms provide a better way for users to enter data into your database. Rather than work through the Access interface and type data directly into tables, you can provide data-entry forms that will guide users through the process.

The easiest way of generating a form is using the AutoForm Wizard. The form it creates can then be modified to suit your requirements.

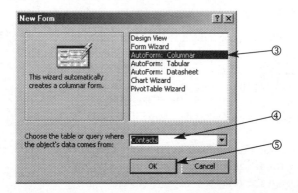

1 In the database window, click on the **Forms** object.

2 Click on the New button.

3 Click on **AutoForm: Columnar**.

4 Select a table or query in the drop-down box at the bottom of the New Form dialog box.

5 Click on **OK**.

A form is created with all the fields from the table and an entry box of suitable size in each case. When you close the form you are given the opportunity to save it.

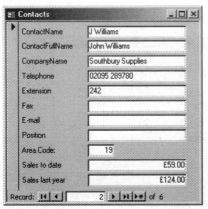

Create a form for entering multiple records

You can use the AutoForm Wizard to create a tabular form, with one row of entry boxes for each record. This allows users to type in several records in the same form.

1 In the database window, click on the **Forms** object.

2 Click on the ⊞ New button.

3 Click on **AutoForm: Tabular**.

4 Select a table or query in the drop-down box at the bottom of the New Form dialog box.

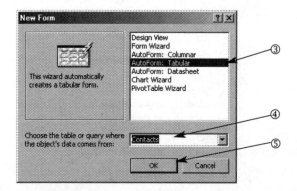

5 Click on **OK**.

A form is created with all the fields from the table as column headings and an entry box of suitable size in each case. When you close the form you are given the opportunity to save it.

	Contactf	ContactF	Company	Telephor	Extensior	Fax	E-mail		Position	de:	is to date	es last year
►	J K Evar	John K E	Evans &	07908 2(						15	£45.00	£0.00
	J William	John Wil	Southbu	02095 2(	242					19	£59.00	£124.00
	M Evans	Mark Ev.	Southbu	02095 2(	297					19	£100.00	£90.00
	N James	Nigella J.	DSR	02095 6!						12	£32.00	£16.00
	R Fletch	Ron Fleti	New Wc	02095 5!						14	£50.00	£75.00
	T Smith	Tom Smi	ABC Elei	02095 3;						19	£77.00	£76.00
*										99	£0.00	£0.00

Record: I◄ ◄   1 ► ►I ►* of 6

You can also create a form that looks like Datasheet view and may therefore be easier to read than the tabular form. When creating the form, select AutoForm: Datasheet.

Create a form using the Form Wizard

For more control over a form than is offered by the AutoForm Wizard, use the Form Wizard.

1 In the database window, click on the **Forms** object.

2 Click on the ⊞New button.

3 Click on **Form Wizard**.

4 Select a table or query in the drop-down box at the bottom of the New Form dialog box.

5 Click on **OK**.

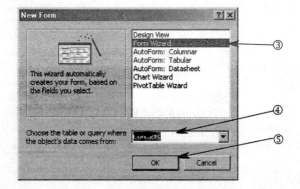

6 Choose the fields to be shown on the form using the buttons in the middle of the dialog box. Click on the top button to add the field to the form or the button below to add all fields. The other two buttons remove one or all fields from the form. Repeat this process with other tables and fields, if required. Click on **Next**.

>	Add selected field
>>	Add all fields
<	Remove selected field
<<	Remove all fields

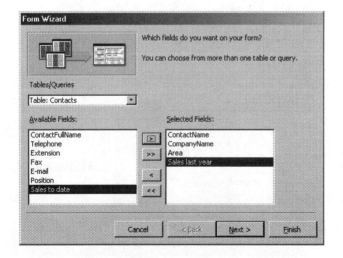

7 Choose the layout for the form. The standard layouts are similar to those produced by the AutoForm Wizard.

8 Select a style for the text, boxes and background of the form.

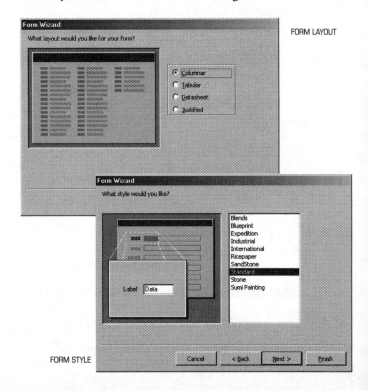

FORM LAYOUT

FORM STYLE

9 Type a name for the form, choose whether to view or edit the form, and click on **Finish**.

The form is generated and can now be used for data entry.

CREATING FORMS

Edit a form

In Design view, you can edit a form that has been created by a wizard. You can also use Design view for creating forms from scratch.

1 In the database window, click on the **Forms** object.

2 Click on the form and then on the ≥ Design button.

3 Make the changes to the form design.

4 Close the Design view and save the changes.

Turn off the grid lines

When you open a form in Design view, grid lines are displayed in the background. Although these can be helpful in lining up objects on the form, it is often easier to work with a form when they are turned off.

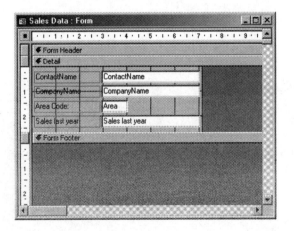

To turn the grid lines off, click on **Grid** on the **View** menu.

You can use the same option to turn the grid lines on again later, if required.

Change the form size

The form is divided into three sections.

• You can change the size of any of these sections by dragging the dividing lines between them.

• You can change the size of the form by dragging its right and bottom edges.

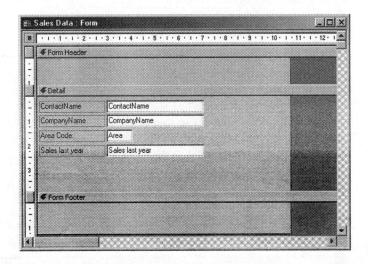

Use the form sections

The form's three sections can be adapted to suit your own requirements:

- The Form Header section is usually used for title text.

- The Detail section usually contains the fields themselves.

- The Form Footer section is usually reserved for command buttons (such as **OK** and **Cancel**).

You can, of course, use these sections for any other purposes.

Move form objects

The form contains a number of objects. Initially, these are just the field entry boxes with their associated labels; later, you may add other objects, such as text labels and option buttons.

You can move any object to a new position by placing the mouse pointer over the object and then dragging the object to a new position.

Change object properties

Each object on the form has a number of properties that affect the way it appears on the form and the way it behaves. You can change any of these properties.

1 Right-click on an object.

2 Select **Properties** from the pop-up menu.

3 The properties are grouped under a number of tabs. Click on a tab to see properties of a particular type.

4 To change a property, click on the text box to the right of the property and either enter a new value or select a value from a drop-down list (depending on the type of property).

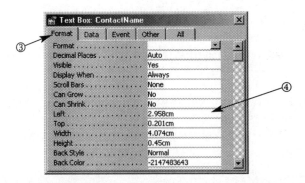

Add an object to the form

The Design view for forms has a Toolbox, which contains a number of objects that can be added to a form (called *controls*).

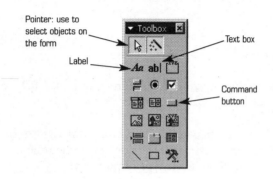

Pointer: use to select objects on the form

Text box

Label

Command button

To add an object:

1 Click on the required control type on the Toolbox.

2 Drag the pointer to mark out the area for the control on the form.

3 If the control contains any text (e.g. a label), type the text directly.

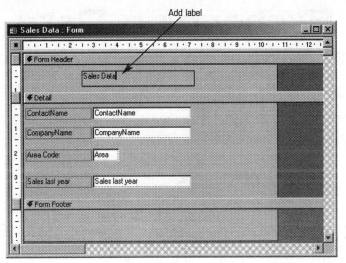

Add label

4 Change any other relevant properties for the control.

Add a field to a form

To add a field:

1 Add a suitable control to the form.

2 In the control's properties, click on the **Data** tab and select the field in the **Control Source** property.

Exchanging Data

Import data

You can import existing data into Access from a number of
sources: for example, a formatted text file, a comma separated
variables file or an Excel worksheet.

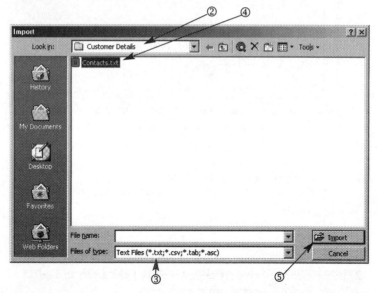

1 From the **File** menu, select **Get External Data** and **Import**.

2 The Import box is displayed. Find the directory where the data is held.

3 In the **Files of type** box select the relevant group of files.

4 Click on the file to be imported.

5 Click on **Import**.

The way in which the import proceeds depends on the type of file that has been selected.

Import an Excel worksheet

A table can be imported from an Excel worksheet, provided it has been formatted appropriately.

1 From the **File** menu, select **Get External Data** and **Import**.

2 Find the directory and file (of type 'xls'), and click on **Import**.

3 Follow the instructions on screen (which are similar to those for the import of CSV and text files: see page 235).

Import an Access database

To import tables from another Access database:

1 From the **File** menu, select **Get External Data** and **Import**.

2 Find the directory and file (of type 'mdb'), and click on **Import**.

3 Click on the fields to be imported.

4 Click on **OK**.

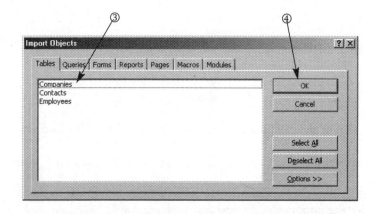

Import a CSV or text file

Comma separated values files consist of a file of text in which
each line represents a single record. The data in the line is
separated by a comma, with each item between the commas
being the value for one field.

To import a CSV or text file:

1 From the **File** menu, select **Get External Data** and **Import**.

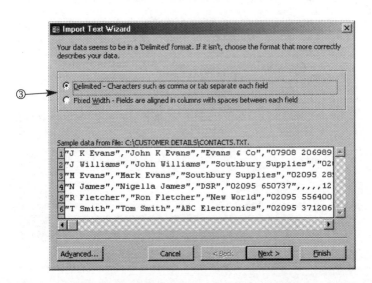

③

2 Find the directory and file (of type 'txt' or 'csv'), and click on **Import**.

3 Select the option depending on whether the file is a delimited (CSV) file or a formatted text file, with the text in fixed width columns. The file you are importing is shown in the lower part of the dialog box. Click on **Next**.

4 Click on the character used to separate fields (usually either a comma or a tab). If the first line of the file contains any sort of

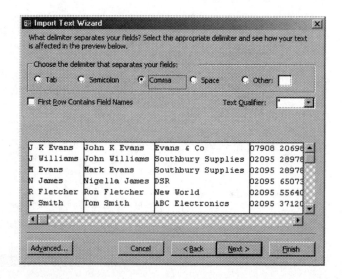

headings, rather than data, click on the **First Row Contains Field Names** check box. Specify the character used to enclose text items (usually double quote marks). Click on **Next**.

5 Specify whether the data is to go in a new table or an existing table. If an existing table, select the table from the drop-down list. Click on **Next**.

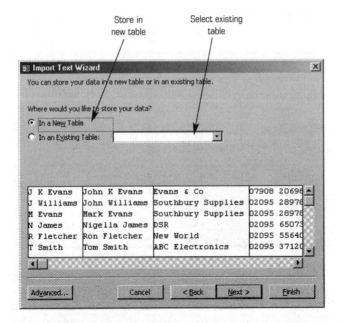

Store in new table

Select existing table

6 Click on each field in turn. Enter a name for the field, identify the data type and specify whether or not the field is to be indexed. Alternatively, click on **Do not import field** if you do not want to import the data in that column. When all the fields have been identified, click on **Next**.

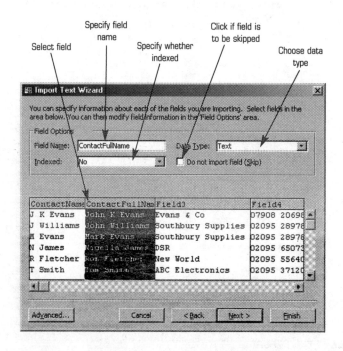

7 Either allow Access to assign a primary key field (and automatically number the records) or choose a primary key from the list of fields. Click on **Next**.

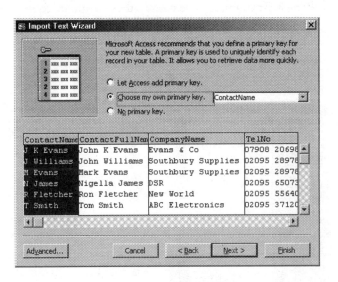

8 Give the table a name. Decide whether you want to analyse the table in Design view after it has been imported. Click on **Finish**. The table is imported and can be opened in Datasheet view.

Export a database

Tables in Access databases can be exported to almost any other Windows program.

1 In the database window, click on the table to be exported.

2 From the **File** menu, select **Export**.

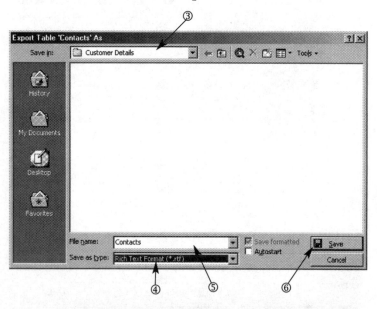

3 Locate the directory where the file is to be placed.

4 Select the type of file to be created (for example, a text file, an Excel worksheet or, for export to Word, an RTF file).

5 Enter a filename.

6 Click on **Save**.

The file is exported to the selected file type.

DATA EXPORTED TO A TABLE IN WORD (VIA RTF FORMAT)

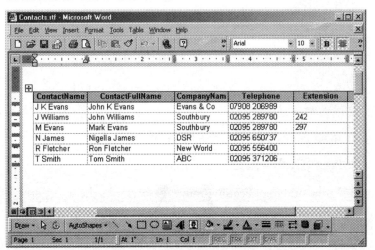

Cut and paste data from other applications

You can copy data from most Windows applications using the cut-and-paste method.

1 In the Windows application, mark a block of data of a suitable format.

2 Press **[Ctrl]** + **[C]**.

3 In Access, open a table and mark a block of the correct size.

4 Press **[Ctrl]** + **[V]**.

Copy data to other applications

You can copy data from Access to most other Windows applications.

1 In an Access table, mark a block of data.

2 Press **[Ctrl]** + **[C]**.

3 In the other application, move the cursor to the insertion point.

4 Press **[Ctrl]** + **[V]**.